I0528978

The Harriet Tubman Way

An Inspirational Guide to Self-Love,
Empowerment, and Legendary
Leadership for Girls

KAROL V. BROWN

THE HARRIET TUBMAN WAY

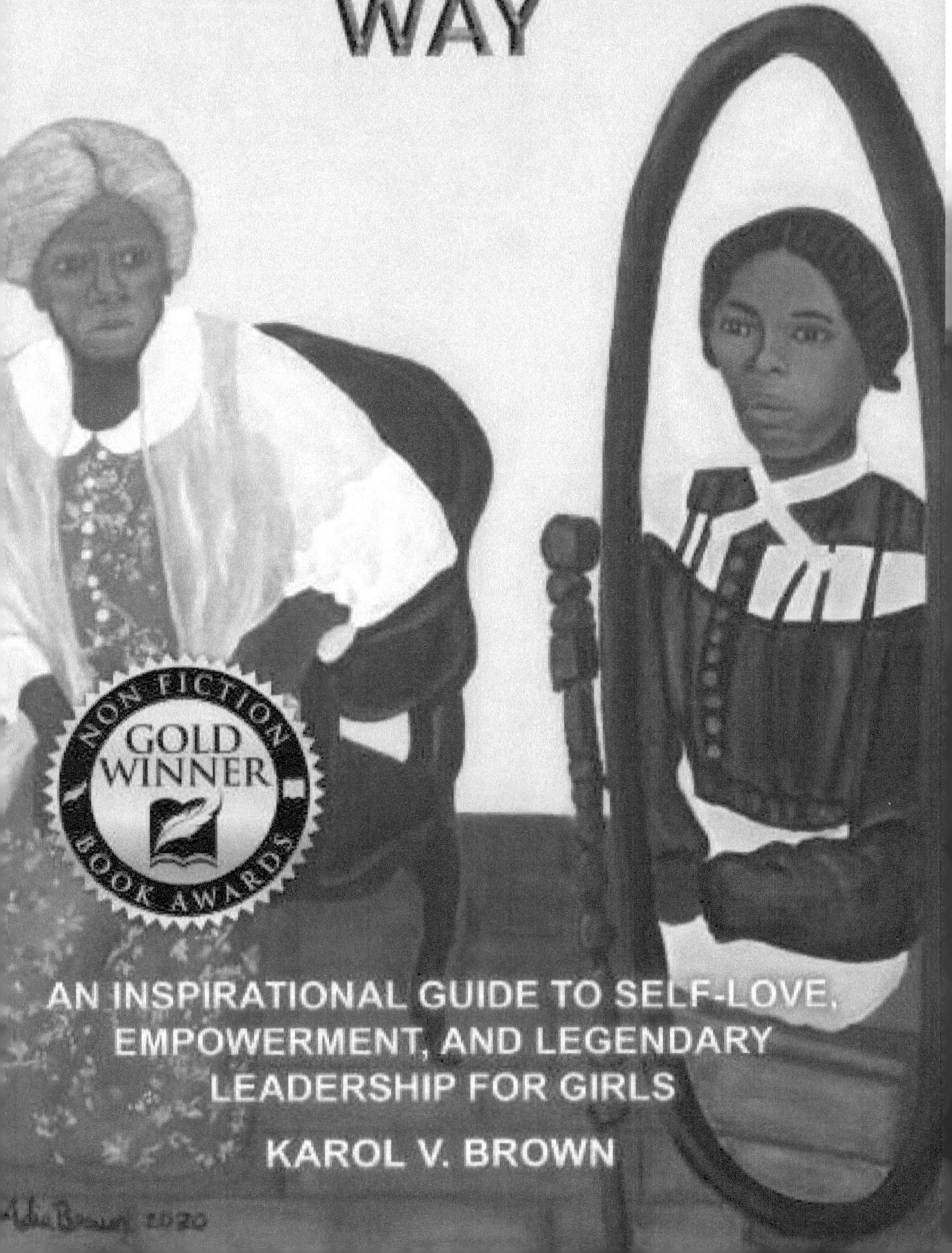

AN INSPIRATIONAL GUIDE TO SELF-LOVE, EMPOWERMENT, AND LEGENDARY LEADERSHIP FOR GIRLS

KAROL V. BROWN

Copyright © 2023 by KAROL V. BROWN

All rights reserved. No parts of this book may be used or reproduced by any means, graphic, electronic, and mechanical, including photocopying, recording, taping, or by any information storage retrieval system, without the written permission of the publisher except in the case of brief quotations embodied in critical articles and reviews.

ISBN: 978-1-961677-20-3 (Paperback)

Library of Congress Control Number: 2023915166

Printed in the United States of America

Published by

info@thequippyquill.com
(302) 295-2278

Contents

DEDICATION

**I dedicate this book to my children and grandchildren
Adia, Ariessunna, Atiara,
Aurmahn, Nathaniel, Moussa, Jamieson, and Aviana
And to all the girls of all ages that read this book**

Acknowledgments

I want to thank all the women in my life who have supported me.

A special thanks to my daughter Adia Brown who painted Harriet Tubman Reflecting

Figure 1 https://www.facebook.com/adiapaints1/

Book cover art
Harriet Tubman Reflecting by Adia Brown

PREFACE

Harriet Tubman is known as a woman with courage, bravery, and compassion, and because of these qualities, she is recognized as a legendary leader. As a conductor on the Underground Railroad, she is known for freeing herself from slavery in Maryland and returning thirteen times to free family and friends. There are many books and several movies sharing her story of the challenges, sacrifices, and dangers she faced to free her people. How did she do it? Was she born with superpowers? Well, she could not do any of the fantastic feats you might see on a superhero movie, but I do believe she was born with a spirit of super people.

Her superpowers were not something you could see when you looked at her. What she had was within her, the spirit that was her birthright. A birthright that came from her parents and her African roots. She was a black girl who had a dream for herself. A big dream of freedom.

Fortunately for us, Sarah H. Bradford interviewed Harriet Tubman as an elderly woman and published her life stories, *Scenes in the life of Harriet Tubman*. As a storyteller portraying Harriet Tubman, I learned the stories in Sarah Bradford's book well enough to get an understanding of how the stories are lessons. *The Harriet Tubman Way: An Inspirational Guide to Self-Love, Empowerment, and Legendary Leadership for Girls* shares lessons I learned from Harriet Tubman's life. Each story is written as if you were hearing the stories from Harriet herself.

Harriet Tubman's stories are inspirational and empowering. Harriet Tubman was named Araminta Ross. Her nickname was Minty. Minty was not born a leader. She was not known for being smart, pretty, or super talented in any particular skills. She was black, poor, and illiterate, plus a victim of physical and mental abuse from slave owners. A severe head injury at about age thirteen left her with an added hardship of uncontrollable sleeping spells. Her sleeping spells could be called narcolepsy, which is considered a handicap today. Minty was doomed by society to live a life in slavery.

How is it she overcame all of these challenges? She had the "spirit of a leader." She had dreams of a better life for herself and her people. Harriet believed she had the right to live a life as a free woman. She loved herself enough to never give up on her dreams. Love is powerful.

Most people have someone they love. Everyone should love themselves. Yet too many girls do not love themselves.

These girls grow up to be women who have suffered from the lack of loving themselves. Their money, energy, and time is spent trying to be what they think is prettier. They hide their smartness because they think it is not attractive. They suffer from allowing others to disrespect them. Their childhood passion and dreams are forgotten. These dreams are unfulfilled because they don't think they have what is needed to be the woman they wanted to be.

This book was written to speak hope, love, and empowerment to all young girls while they are forming their dreams. Like Minty Ross, every girl has an inner super spirit. Anything one puts their total belief and dedication to do, can be realized. When obstacles get in the way, remember Harriet Tubman's famous quote: "Never Give Up!"

The Tubman Way to Legendary Servant Leadership

When Harriet decided to free herself, that was a life-changing decision. She then was compelled to help other people find freedom and the opportunity for a better life. People followed Harriet and she became a leader, not because she set a goal to be a leader, but because she set a goal to serve others. Harriet Tubman's leadership style can be considered servant leadership. Leading through service to others is servant leadership.

This concept of service to others can be traced back as far as the Bible. Jesus taught his disciples that one who serves others is greater than the one being served (Luke 22:27). The parable of the Good Samaritan is another example of servant leadership (Luke 10:30-35). This story teaches us that everyone should be considered a neighbor that we should love and help. The concept of love thy neighbor is not just found in the Christian religion; love and service to others is universal.

A more recent concept of servant leadership was presented in the 1970s by Robert K. Greenleaf. Mr. Greenleaf created the phrase "servant leadership." The focus of servant leaders is on the growth and well-being of people and the communities to which they belong.

How do you figure out if someone is a servant leader? Mr. Greenleaf presents the "Best Test" for servant leaders. I have used this test to examine Harriet Tubman's life. Look at these four questions on this test with me while you think of what you know about Harriet Tubman.

1. Do those serve grow as persons?
2. Do they, while being served, become healthier, wiser, freer, more independent, or free, more likely themselves to become servants?

3.   What is the effect on the least privileged in society?
4.   Will they benefit, or at least, will they not be further deprived?

Now let's look at Harriet Tubman's life. Did the people Harriet Tubman serve grow as persons? Did they become healthier, wiser? Did the people who were the least privileged in society benefit from Harriet Tubman's service and leadership? I say YES to all four questions. The people rescued by Harriet Tubman were able to grow in many ways.

1.   We do know they were freer. They were free to educate themselves and their children. This education supplied the knowledge needed for their children to raise themselves out of poverty.
2.   They could now work and earn their own money. With money, they were able to supply clothing, food, and housing for their families.
3.   The people Harriet Tubman served, and their children and grandchildren lead the way for black business owners, city officials, and educators who serve their communities as leaders.

Here are some examples of Harriet Tubman as a leader. Harriet Tubman was a:

- Community leader. After freeing herself, she returned to her community to rescue approximately seventy people, including her parents and brothers.
- Social justice collaborator. As a conductor on the Underground Railroad, she partnered with a network of people working to rescue others who were living in an unjust society.
- Military leader. Served as a spy, and a scout for the United States Army in the Civil War, she was the first woman in the US Army to organize and lead a raid that freed over 750 people in one day.

- Nurse. Serving in the Civil War, she used her knowledge of herbal medicine to cure hundreds of people from dysentery, (an intestinal infection that causes bloody diarrhea).
- Engaging teacher and businesswoman. During the Civil War, she taught women how to start businesses such as a laundry that cleaned soldiers' uniforms and bakers that sold their product.
- Compassionate caregiver. She established a home for poor and homeless people in Auburn, New York.
- Public speaker. She traveled as an abolitionist before the war telling stories about her life. Later she spoke on civil and human rights at the Women's Rights Conventions.
- Founding member of the National Association of Colored Women (NACWC).

Harriet Tubman's leadership traits are based on her personality, her experiences, and the spirit of service. These are skills that we will share in this book.

How to Use This Book

This book is divided into three parts: Part One: Love In Actions, Part Two: Self-Empowerment, and Part Three: Legendary Leadership.

Along with Harriet Tubman's stories, this book shares quotes from other leaders that dreamed big. The quotes are from people many readers will recognize by name.

I encourage readers to research these leaders and to learn their stories. The inclusion of many examples of people who are leaders in various fields inspires readers to realize that anyone can step up, stand for something, step out, and take the lead to make a difference. You can be the one. The power of one comes from within you. Just as the beautiful voice of Whitney Huston told us in the last line the song, "The Greatest Love of All", "Find your strength in love". Self-love empowers your strength.

Self-love and self-empowerment are the superpowers that can transform a person's life. We want girls to learn about their superpowers early in life. Harriet Tubman is a role model for girls. We know the outcome of her story. We can learn from her as we learn about her.

Life stories are full of lessons. You can learn from your own life. As you get older and reflect on the woman in the mirror, remember the girl you were and how and what you have achieved.

Use The Harriet Tubman Way: An Inspirational Guide to Self-Love, Empowerment, and Legendary Leadership for Girls Journal. Keep it and use it. Write down your thoughts, your experiences, and questions you have to answer along your path.

Learning is ongoing and we can learn from our own observations, listening, and using thinking skills. The inspiration to learn how to become the person you want to be, is empowered when you use your imagination to visualize the world you want for those you love, including yourself. When you reflect on your writings, you will realize that you also have a story to share.

This is a book for an individual to read, but it is designed to generate both self-reflection, group discussion, and active service-based learning. Girls are encouraged to use their developing skills in communication, creativity, critical thinking, and collaboration to discover they, too, can be a legendary leader.

To enhance your experience of learning from Harriet Tubman and other leaders, take the time to visit the websites suggested in the book.

If you are reading from a physical book, there are QR codes for you to easily visit sites as you read. At our website there are links to meditations, affirmations, songs and quotes.

Visit and get access to videos at www.karolvbrown.com

How to use this book:

www.karolvbrown.com

Part One

Love In Actions

You deserve to be happy; you deserve to be joyful; you deserve to be celebrated. But in order to do that you must first fall madly in love with yourself.

—*Lisa Nichols*

For Minty, a small, sickly, and timid little girl, to become Harriet Tubman, a free woman that is known for her courage and compassionate leadership, she had to realize that she deserved a better life. She learned to love herself. Self-love is a concept that many girls struggle with as they mature. All of the images of perfection of beauty, talents, and achievements of others can blur the image of one's own attributes. Every person born has their unique beauty, purpose, and worthiness to be loved and respected. This is not a lesson just from Harriet Tubman. Do an internet search for songs about self-love. You will find songs from all types of singing styles with this message: "love yourself."

With the power that comes from love, there are no boundaries of what you can do. Love is the answer. When you love other people, you care about their safety, health, living conditions, and how others treat them. This love does not have to be limited to your own family. Love of all people builds the community that will hold us together.

Harriet Tubman's stories are examples of what Love In Actions means. Love is not just a word that is hard to describe; it is the responsibility that powers actions. Love In Actions is rooted in caring for the well-being or love of oneself and all others—people, animals, and the planet.

Figure 3 Elderly Harriet Tubman, also called Aunt Harriet

Chapter 1

Love Yourself First

When I was around eighteen, I looked in the mirror and said, "You're either going to love yourself or hate yourself." And I decided to love myself. That changed a lot of things.

—Queen Latifah

Save Yourself First!

I was born about 1820 or 1821, I ain't sure, because there were no papers to tell my birth date. My mama said it was in the spring of the year, about March. We lived on the Eastern Shores of Maryland in Dorchester County. My name when I was born was Araminta Ross. People called me Minty for short. My daddy's name was Benjamin Ross, we called him Daddy Ben. My mama's name was Harriet Green. When I was about twenty-four years old, I changed my name to Harriet, like my mama. There were nine of us children. I was in the middle. Daddy Ben worked for the Baltimore shipyard as a lumberman. He taught me all kinds of things about the woods, where to hide, which berries were good to eat, and which ones were for medicines. Mama worked in the big house as a cook.

My master hired me out to work away from my parents when I was a young child, about five or six years old. I worked long hours, and I had to grow up fast. When I was away from my family, the people I worked for yelled at me or whipped me for not doing my work right or just for being me.

It was hard on me not to be heartbroken and sad all the time. My master was always sending me to work for some mean folks. When I didn't work out for them, they sent me back home. Then after I got to feeling better with my family, the master would send me to work for some folks meaner than the others were.

When I was home, I felt like somebody worth being treated kindly and that somebody loved me. Sleeping with my mama in her bed made me feel warm and safe. Mama didn't have a bed, just a quilt on the floor. But I was always as close to her on the floor to sleep as I could be. I loved my family, and their love is what I held on to. In my heart, I always had Mama's praying and cooking, Daddy's singing and stories, and my sister and brothers laughing and playing with me. When I was away from my folks and alone on a cold hard floor, just thinking about them helped me feel better. All I could do to comfort myself was think of my family, sing, and pray to Jesus. The only joy in my life was my family. So, I asked Jesus to keep me near my family, always. Well, he brought me through those hard times. Those mean people could not break my spirit.

See, my grandmother's name was Modesty, she was born in Africa. She told us stories about being free and how we come from strong, smart, and loving people. Kings and queens. I held on to what my parents had taught me. We are all part of a chain of people. My grandmother connected me to my people from long ago. I had the spirit of leaders, queens and kings in my blood. They always told me, one day, life will be better.

I believed them. But it sure took a long time to come. I loved myself enough to know, I had the right to be free and when I got a chance to leave, I left to save myself.

You see, you have to take actions to save yourself before you can save anybody else. Love In Actions. Remember that saying. Love In Actions.

Love Yourself First

Hold on to pleasant thoughts. Harriet Tubman's childhood was heartbreaking. She suffered from physical and mental abuse. However, she had something to hold on to when there was no one around to protect her: love. Love comes from who you are inside, we call this your spirit or your soul. Feeling positive about yourself even when life is hard is important to self-love and self-care.

Fortunately, Minty had the love of her family. When there is no particular person to hold on to, there is faith in one's strong unbreakable spirit. This strong spirit is part of one's personality. Your future is dependent on how you feel about yourself. Love yourself first. Love yourself enough to believe you can achieve your biggest dreams.

Activities

Discussion questions:

1. Queen Latifah (Dana Elaine Owens), was born on March 18, 1970. She is an American singer-songwriter, rapper, actress, and producer.

There are two versions of Queen Latifah's song U.N.I.T.Y

1. Watch both versions:
   a. Queen Latifah's "U.N.I.T.Y." 2014 Nobel Peace Prize Concert: https://youtu.be/twv4PP4QSPM
   b. The Official Music Video for U.N.I.T.Y: https://youtu.be/f8cHxydDb7o?si=wL9STxG2h6eYQja9

Discuss the song, both versions and the message to both girls and guys. Has the need for this song message changed?

2. When times are difficult and you are sad, hurt, or your spirit is down, what do you have to hold on to? What thoughts can make you feel better?

Queen Latifah U.N.I.T.Y for Noble Peace

Lisa Nichols was born in 1966, She is an American business owner, bestselling author, and award-winning motivational speaker. She went from a poor single mother to a multimillionaire.

1. Review her quote at the beginning of Part One of this book about loving yourself. What do you think about this quote?
2. Read Lisa Nichols remarkable story of how she went from a single mother with no money for diapers to a multimillion-dollar business owner at:

https://www.motivatingthemasses.com/

Journaling:

1. Write down your name. Now list what you love to do that always makes you feel happy. Revisit this list when you are feeling down.
2. Start with writing some affirmations. An affirmation is a positive statement that you read daily to help you believe the statement about yourself. Post affirmations in places that you look at every day, such as your mirror, or set a daily reminder on your phone calendar to send you an affirmation.

Get creative:

1. Visit our website: www.karolvbrown.com You will find a list of affirmations to get you started with your own list. Use these words in your artwork.
2. Draw, write, or make something to beautify the positive things you love about yourself. Keep it where you can see it daily. Share what you have created.

Chapter 2

Survive and Make Changes

"I can't get mad at my past, but I need more happiness in my future. I want better, I need better & I deserve Better. I can do better if I start with me. So, I'm going to get my ISH together. Change my life & start living better Because I Deserve Better."

— Shanel Cooper Skyes

A Life-Changing Event

One day something happened that changed my life forever. It was in the fall of the year; we called it pickin' time. I was working with a man named Jim. He was a tall, strong-looking man with big arms and a broad chest. Because he was so big and strong, the overseers worked Jim extra hard. Because he worked so hard, he was always talking about running away. Now, y'all know, we couldn't talk out in the open about anything. The overseers would think we were talking about Nat Turner and rising up to kill them. So, we had to sing instead of talk. "Steal Away to Jesus" was Jim's favorite song.

One day Jim seemed restless. He kept his eyes on the overseers more than on his work. He was singing "Steal Away to Jesus" over and over. Then about evening time, the overseers went into the barn to have their supper. As soon as the barn doors closed, Jim threw down his hoe and said, "I am leaving this place."

I kept my eyes on Jim. What did he mean? Before I could figure out what he meant, I heard the barn door open. One of the overseers came out of the barn. He saw Jim headed down the road and said, "Hey boy, get back here!" Jim started running, and the overseer followed Jim down the road. I was scared for Jim, so I followed the overseer. We ended up down at the Bucktown store.

It was getting dark. The door was open, and the moonlight shone just inside the door. I stood in the doorway. There were two other slaves in the store. The overseer had Jim cornered. He was trying to get the other men to grab Jim so he could tie him up and beat him. He saw me peek my head in the door and said, "Stop him, and don't let him get out that door!" I saw Jim run for the door, and I moved out of his way. Y'all know I wasn't going to stop that man from running away! Jim ran past me out the door, and the overseer picked up a two-pound lead weight and threw it at the doorway trying to hit Jim. It hit me instead, hard in the head and just over my eye. I hit the ground, knocked out and bleeding.

You know they don't call a doctor for a little slave girl. They took me to my mama's cabin where I laid near dead on some rags. I remember Mama and others praying and crying. Daddy got some herbs, mashed them up, and put them on my head. They did all they could do. All the time I was lying there, I was praying to have my strength back and to be well again. God heard my prayers. I got my strength back, but I have never been the same since that day. Folks say they seen a change in me. I became more determined to have a different life other than slavery.

Survive and Make Changes

Love and a feeling of responsibility for other people can give you the courage to stand up for someone else. Being an advocate for others is servant leadership. Have faith, stay strong and determined, and you can survive and do extremely well.

Harriet survived the injury that crushed her skull and resulted in a life-long suffering from sleep spells. Today this is called narcolepsy.

This unfortunate event strengthened her commitment to change her life. She became determined to change her destiny. In changing her own life, she changed the lives of many others.

There are often drastic incidents that become life-changing experiences. Sometimes being an advocate for others develops out of your experiences, or of what you see happening to others.

Activities

Discussion questions:

1. Do you know someone who has overcome some difficulties? How are they handling the situation?
2. How can your observations of others dealing with difficulties be used as motivation for you to keep on going?

Journaling:

Shanel Cooper Sykes is an American life coach, author, and speaker. She was born on June 7, 1983, in Brooklyn, New York, USA.

1. Shanel Cooper Sykes is a motivational speaker, author, and life coach known for her work in personal development and empowerment. What is personal development?
2. Write about how you think your career choice would help you in your life's journey.

Research:

Find an organization that stands for what you feel strongly enough about to support. Write a paragraph about the organization, their purpose, and why you selected them to support. What can you do to support this cause?

Chapter 3

Accept the Person You Are

"What I will say is that what I have learned for myself is that I don't have to be anybody else; and that myself is good enough; and that when I am being true to that self. Then I can avail myself to extraordinary things... You have to allow for the impossible to be possible"

— Lupita Nyong'o

I Take Care of My People

Five hundred miles from Maryland to Canada was a long trip. But, when they passed that Fugitive Slave Law (Fugitive Slave Act of 1850), I wouldn't trust Uncle Sam with my people no longer. I wouldn't take a chance of nobody that came up North to freedom with me would be sent back. I took my folks where I knew they would be free and stay free. So, I had to take them clear up to Canada.

Life was hard in Canada. I was responsible for all these folks I brought up to "the coldest place on earth." That's what my mama called St. Catharines, Ontario. Nothing would grow in the winter and the winters were long. Folks were close to starving and freezing. I did all I could to keep clothes on people's backs and shoes on their feet. I was out begging for money and food from any group that would help. I didn't mind asking for help for folks that needed help. Some of my friends said, "Harriet, you are always asking for help for someone else. What about you? What can I do for you?" I said, "The Lord takes care of me, but I need money to do His work and that is to take care of my people."

I knew I had to find a way to make my mama more comfortable. I prayed about it and after a year in Canada, I was able to move Mama, Daddy, and a couple of more into my own house in

Auburn, New York. Mama still complained, but not about being in, "The coldest place on earth." Both my Mama and Daddy lived to be in their eighties.

I guess my training in the army as a nurse was part of the Lord preparing me to care for people all my life. Back in the war, I worked in the hospital, and I did everything I could do to help those poor souls. My day started early. I'd go to the hospital and get me a big chunk of ice in a basin and fill it up with water. I'd go to the first man, and flies was thick as bees in a hive. I'd wash away the flies and bathe off the wounds. I'd talk and pray with the soldier and then move on to the next one. By the time my ice melted, my water was as red as blood. I'd get another chunk and start over again. I did this all day. The Lord gave me the gift of service and I am glad I could do as He wanted me to do, take care of my people.

I knew I had to find a way to make my mama more comfortable. I prayed about it and after a year in Canada, I was able to move Mama, Daddy, and a couple of more into my own house in Auburn, New York. Mama still complained, but not about being in, "The coldest place on earth." Both my Mama and Daddy lived to be in their eighties.

I guess my training in the army as a nurse was part of the Lord preparing me to care for people all my life. Back in the war, I worked in the hospital, and I did everything I could do to help those poor souls. My day started early. I'd go to the hospital and get me a big chunk of ice in a basin and fill it up with water. I'd go to the first man, and flies was thick as bees in a hive. I'd wash away the flies and bathe off the wounds. I'd talk and pray with the soldier and then move on to the next one. By the time my ice melted, my water was as red as blood. I'd get another chunk and start over again. I did this all day. The Lord gave me the gift of service and I am glad I could do as He wanted me to do, take care of my people.

Accept the Person You Are

Be humble and willing to serve others. Harriet Tubman was a very humble person; she found no shame in being who she was and doing the work she did. Humility is different from humiliation, which is shame and embarrassment. Being humble is feeling or showing respect and admiration toward other people. Being humble also means giving service and taking responsibility for others' needs and comforts before your own. It is a demonstration of being of higher rather than a lower level of character. There is greatness, not weakness, in humility.

Activities

Discussion questions:

Lupita Nyong'o is a Kenyan-Mexican actress and producer. She was born on March 1, 1983, in Mexico City, Mexico.

1. Name 2 of Lupita's movies.
2. Lupita Nyong'o is known not only for her acting talent but also for her advocacy work in promoting diversity and inclusion in the entertainment industry. What is diversity and inclusion?
3. Do you think being of service is being humble, or humiliated?

Journaling:

1. How does being of service to others show greatness?
2. Are there people that you can name who are examples of being humble servants that you admire?

Storytelling:

Tell a short story about a humble person (servant leader) that you admire.

Chapter 4

Practice Forgiveness

For me, the healing process starts with graciousness and forgiveness.

— India Arie

Miss Susan's House

I grew up like a neglected weed. I didn't know anything about freedom. I never learned to read or write. Little slave children didn't go to school. We went to work. Nobody that I worked for and stayed with cared if I was hungry, sick, or cold. I didn't have hardly any clothes and no shoes.

I remember one morning they sent me away as if it were yesterday.

I was about six years old, and it was early in the morning when this white woman came and loaded me in her wagon and took me away. The master told me to call her Miss Susan. I thought for sure this was the last time I would see my family. My master broke my heart. I was scared to death of this evil-looking woman who I thought came to take me down into the Deep South. She wore her hair up in a ball, and she had this wrinkle across her forehead that never went away. She was a mean woman who never smiled. Although she wasn't rich, she had enough money for a young slave. She didn't just want a slave to care for her baby; she wanted someone to clean her house too.

Miss Susan's house was a real house. I had never been in a house before. Where I lived was just an old one-room shack with a dirt floor. In Miss Susan's house, there was a room for everything. She had a room for cooking, a room for eating, rooms for the beds, and they had real beds. Then there was a room for sitting, and she called it the parlor.

Now, folks, when you live in a shack with dirt floors, you don't have much to clean. But Miss Susan thought nothing about the difference between what kind of place I lived in and her house. She said, "Sweep the floor and dust the furniture."

Now when I was leaving, the last thing my mama said was, "Minty, you do what they tell you to do and don't ask questions." I always did what my mama said. So, I tried to do what she ordered me to do without asking how to do it.

When I got finished, Miss Susan came in. She took her finger and wiped it across a table. Then that wrinkle in her head got tighter, and she said, "You stupid girl! Can't you do anything right?" She grabbed her cowhide whip and hit me across my back and arms. I cried, but she didn't care. She said, "Do it over!" I did it over. Miss Susan came back and whipped me for not doing it right. I did it over again and again. She whipped me five times and got meaner with each time. I was getting more and more scared and worried about her killing me.

Then her sister Miss Emily came from upstairs. She had been hearing all the screaming and crying. I don't know how she stood up there listening so long, but I was glad she finally came down. She said, "Susan, what are you doing? Beating her is not going to get the work done right. Don't you think if she knew what to do, she would do it right so that you would stop beating her? Leave her with me." Miss Susan frowned at me and left the room. Miss Emily wasn't so scary. She looked like her sister, but without the wrinkle in her forehead. She told me to show her what I was doing. Then when she saw what I was doing wrong, she said, "Open the window and sweep the floor. Then go to the dining room and set the table for breakfast. Come back and wipe off the tables." That is what I did, and it worked.

Miss Susan never acted sorry for being stupid herself. But, you know, she didn't know any better. Her folks taught her that slaves are dumb and that you have to beat them to make them work like animals.

Now that woman was going to make sure she got her money's worth of work out of me. If I was not cleaning the house, I was sitting somewhere holding her baby. At night, I had to keep the baby asleep by rocking his cradle. Now, if I fell asleep and stopped rocking, the baby would wake up. If he cried and woke his mother, I was in trouble. His mother had her whip by her bed, so she did not have to reach far to get it. She would take that whip and hit me around my neck. Oh, I tell you, I was so scared of her, I would shake whenever she came into the room.

When they sent me back to my mama, I was a shaky bag of bones—crying all the time, with nothing but bad stories to tell about Miss Susan. But Mama and Daddy helped me understand that I would survive this horrible experience. Mama taught me to forgive Miss Susan. She said if I hold on to my feelings of wanting to get back at Miss Susan for what she did to me, I would be keeping myself from feeling better. So, I let it go and forgave her. I am glad I did that. I ain't got no time for bad thoughts to slow me down.

Practice Forgiveness

Forgive and have faith. To overcome negative experiences, you must free your mind of any bitterness. Forgiveness allows your mind to let go of the bad thoughts and brings you peace. Forgiveness is the first step to overcoming the past. Have faith that there will be better days ahead. Forgiveness is another way to express love.

Activities

Discussion questions:

India Arie Simpson was born October 3, 1975, also known as India Arie is an American singer and songwriter.

1. Find India Arie's song "Worthy" on her album named "Worthy". Discuss the words to this song and what they mean to you.

Journaling:

1. If you are angry at someone, write them a letter telling them why you are angry and how they make you feel. When you are finished, read it, tear it out of your journal, and throw it in the trash. Make this the point of starting to forgive.

2. Write yourself a love letter. Highlight the person you are or want to be. List how you can be "the one" that does something to change your community.

Practice Positive Thoughts:

Review your creation from the first lesson and remember to keep your spirit strong and loving yourself.

Chapter 5

Imagine Your Freedom

Don't let anyone rob you of your imagination, your creativity, or your curiosity. It's your place in the world; it's your life. Go on and do all you can with it, and make it the life you want to live.

— Mae Jemison

Joe Couldn't Imagine Freedom

I was twenty-nine years old before I left Maryland and found a new world just a few miles away. The route I took to freedom started from Maryland. I left there and crossed over into Delaware, and then to Pennsylvania. Next, I traveled through New Jersey and New York. When they passed that Fugitive Slave Law, there was no safety except under the paw of the British Lion. I started traveling all the way to Canada; I had to go into another country to stay free.

To get to Canada, I took a train across a bridge that went over the Niagara Falls. That was a beautiful sight, but not as beautiful as what was on the other side—freedom!

I remember one trip when I took Joe across the bridge. Joe was a big, strong, hardworking young man. His master hired him out to another man for six years. The man who hired him decided to buy Joe. He paid $1,000 up front for Joe and promised to pay $1,000 more on time.

The first thing he did after buying Joe was whip him. He said he wanted to let Joe know who his owner and boss was now. Joe was in shock. He had done his best work for this man, and this is how he treated him. Joe was not going to stay around to be mistreated. He got word to my family that the next time Moses came to town, he was leaving with her. Joe and six other people left with me on that next trip back North.

It was a hard trip; Joe's owner put up a big reward for him and the patrollers were out in force. We had to scatter for a while and meet up in different places. It took us two weeks to make the hundred-mile trip to Wilmington, Delaware. When we finally got to Mr. Thomas Garrett's house in Wilmington, he already knew about Joe. Mr. Garrett had a plan to get us across a guarded bridge in the false bottom of two wagons, which looked like wagons full of bricks. No one would expect people were lying under bricks.

We got through the next 130 miles to New York. Do you know when we got to Mr. Oliver Johnson's place in New York City, he recognized Joe from the reward posters? First thing Mr. Johnson said was, "Well, I'm glad to see the man whose head is worth $1,500." Why did he say that? Joe's heart sank. It took us over two weeks to get to New York City and they were looking for him all the way up here. When he found out we still had four hundred miles to go and then cross a suspension bridge to get to Canada, Joe let his fear get the best of him. Joe gave up. He just knew he was going back to slavery and to the whip of that evil man. He hardly said anything, he would not eat or sing with us anymore. He just sat with his head in his hands. When we got on the train from Niagara Falls headed across the bridge into Canada, the group started singing and jumping for joy. But not Joe, he was still silent. I always thought looking down at the falls was a special welcome to freedom. I always wanted everyone to look. I said, "Joe, come look at the falls! Joe, you old fool, come see the falls! It's your last chance." Joe sat still and never raised his head. Then when we got to the center of the bridge, we had crossed the line from New York into Canada, a free country. I sprang across to Joe's seat, shook him with all my might, and said, "Joe, we've crossed the line!" Joe don't know what I'm talking about. "Joe, you're free!" Finally, Joe knew what I was talking about; his face lit up, and he was shouting, crying, and singing all at the same time.

Joe sang, "Glory to God and Jesus too, one more soul is safe! Oh, go and carry the news, one more soul got safe."

I said, "Joe, come and look at the falls!" He just kept singing.

When the train stopped on the other side, Joe's feet were the first after the conductors to touch British soil. Folks, I tell you it was quite a day! The waters of Niagara were roaring, and I could still hear Joe singing in the background when I welcomed everyone to freedom. Other folks on the train thought he was crazy, but Joe was just full of joy and praising God to be free. Joe said, "Oh! If I'd felt like this down South, it would have taken nine men to take me away from there. Only one more journey for me now and that is to Heaven!"

I said, "Well, you old fool, you might have looked at the falls first, and then gone to Heaven afterwards." Hee-hee.

Children, when you travel, take time to enjoy the sights and the people. When you travel, you get to learn how other folks live. If it is different than how you live, you then know that there is more than one way to live. Joe lived to be a free man because he was willing to travel to a new place.

Imagine Your Freedom

Whenever you can, travel. Appreciate nature, and enrich the life experience by meeting new people, seeing new places, and trying new foods. Being free in mind and body allows you to explore life beyond what you can see outside your front door.

While traveling and portraying Harriet Tubman, I have met many people I would have never met. I have learned more history about the state I live in just by visiting the libraries and schools around the state. I have many more great acquaintances and some new friends. It is through finding out about other places that you can evaluate your own environment. Maybe there is a better place for you, or maybe you will learn to appreciate where you are even more.

Activities

Discussion questions:

Mae Carol Jemison was born October 17, 1956. She is an American engineer, physician, and former NASA astronaut. She became the first African-American woman to travel into space when she served as a mission specialist aboard the Space Shuttle Endeavour in 1992.

1. Mae Jemison was an astronaut, what other titles and careers has she had?

Journaling:

1. Where would you go if you could go anywhere in the world?
2. Visit your dream location vicariously (by reading a book, visiting a website, or watching a travel show).

Be creative:

Describe in a drawing, poem, story, or song your imaginary wonderful world. You can also make a vision board with pictures of all the places you would like to visit.

Chapter 6

Write and Tell Your Story

If there's a book you really want to read, but it hasn't been written yet, then you must write it.

— Toni Morrison

Sarah Bradford's Books

I have some wonderful friends. When I was having problems paying my mortgage and about to lose my house in Auburn, a woman named Sarah Bradford offered to write a book about me. She said, "Harriet, your life deserves to be documented. I'm sure if I write about you, people will buy the book and you'll have the money you need for your mortgage."

Some days I would go to her house and tell her my stories. Sometimes she came to my house. We would sit for hours, and I told her about how I was treated growing up as a slave in Maryland. About my family and how three of my sisters were sold away on the chain gang down in the Deep South. I told her about some of my trips on the Underground Railroad and my friends that helped me. Miss Sarah said, "Harriet, I believe all your stories because I know you, but your stories are so fascinating that some people reading this book would never believe it."

She wrote letters to some of the stationmasters and my friends asking about my stories. She got letters back from people who said, "If Harriet said it, you can believe it." Some people even said they remembered some of the people in my stories coming through their homes.

Miss Sarah added these letters in the book. In 1869, she published Scenes in the Life of Harriet Tubman. She gave the money she made from it to me to pay off my house.

I told Miss Sarah more stories that she added to the first book. In 1886, she published it with the new title of Harriet Tubman: The Moses of Her People.

The book made its way to England to Queen Victoria. After she heard my stories, she sent me a nice letter and invited me to her Golden Jubilee celebration. I was too old to go by then. I was proud of that letter, and I showed it to folks, but so many handled it that now it's just some blurry writing on thin paper and you can't read it no more.

The queen sent me gifts, too. Imagine me, Harriet Tubman, getting a gift from the Queen of England all because somebody wrote a book about me. She sent me a beautiful silk shawl and a Golden Jubilee medal with her picture on one side and her family on the other.

Telling my stories was one thing I can surely do. So, when folks come and visit, I always love to tell stories.

Write and Tell Your Story

Share your stories. Oral communication is important, and telling stories is a natural way we talk. Harriet Tubman told her stories that we call oral history. If her stories were not written, we would not know as much about her as we do today. To make history, stories should be written down. Storytelling stimulates your mind by making learning more interesting. Interesting learning leads to growth. Read stories and write and tell your own stories. Share your stories with others. Storytelling has become a skill practiced by great leaders who encourage their followers and employees to learn to do. You can start now telling stories, and over time, this skill will help you advance in your goals.

Activities

Discussion question:

Chloe Anthony Wofford Morrison (born Chloe Ardelia Wofford; February 18, 1931 – August 5, 2019), known as Toni Morrison, was an American novelist.

1. What are the names of some of Toni Morrison's books? What does she write about?
2. What could you write about that would be similar to Toni Morrison's style of writing?

Journaling:

1. What is your story? Write a description of one of your memorable days. This is a story about you, your words, and your thoughts.
2. By writing the story, you have documented some of your history. If you find you like writing, continue journaling stories.
3. How can you draw upon personal moments to help others?

Tell your story:

1. Review your story, outline it to have an opening, middle, and ending.
2. Practice telling your story—not reading it. Share your story.

Chapter 7

Demand Respect!

To me, race is not all about grievance. It is also about pride and empathy and humanity and understanding the value of difference. But along with that, there are also expectations that we should set for ourselves and for others. We should expect to be treated as equal citizens.

—Gwen Ifill

Say What Needs to be Said, and Say It the Way You Say It

The fight for freedom, rights, and respect are a constant struggle. It is because there's always someone trying to take your freedom away from you.

I was in Boston at the New England Colored Citizens' Convention. I heard a man speaking about the white folks didn't know what to do with the free colored folks. There was talk about sending us back to Africa. I had to say something about this bad idea.

I listened to the speech, and then I made my way to the stage. They didn't invite me, but they knew if I had something to say, they couldn't stop me from speaking. I looked at the man who just finished and I told him a story.

"There was once a farmer that owned some cows. He sold the milk and had a good business. But he wasn't happy with the amount of money he made off his milk, so he sowed some onions and garlic on his land to get the cows to make more milk. The garlic and onions grew really good. The cows ate them and made more milk. The farmer used the extra milk and made butter and cheese to sell. He soon found that the milk, cheese, and butter tasted like garlic and onions. Folks didn't like it, so he couldn't sell it. He decided to get rid of the garlic and the onions and to sow clover instead. He plowed it up but found that the wind had blown the onions and garlic all over his field. It was deeply rooted, and he couldn't pull it up." I said, "Now mister, that man and his cows is just like how the white folks brought us black folks over here from Africa to do their work. Now that they can't use us no more, they want to uproot us and send us back. Well, you can't do that. We've been here for over two hundred years. We ain't never been in Africa. All of us here now were born here. We built these streets and these great buildings. We grew the crops. We raised white children and our children together, right here in this country. We are rooted here, and we ain't going nowhere! This is our country. We are all Americans." Well, I didn't hear much more from that man.

Demand Respect!

Have courage. Speak up for yourself and others. Take a stance, claim your rights, and demand respect. Use your unique personality and style of communication.

Harriet Tubman was a storyteller. A simple parable can express more than a statement made in anger. She had too much self-respect to let someone else determine her life. Don't let others decide your fate without you giving them your thoughts. Don't be afraid to speak in simple language. Use your own style of communication. It may be through stories, songs, poems, or even drawings that express your deepest feelings. Your creative message may be the best way for people to understand how you and many others feel. Being yourself is the best way to get the results you want.

Activities

Discussion questions:

Gwen Ifill was born on September 29, 1955 and died on November 14, 2016. She was an American journalist, television newscaster, and author.

1. Gwen Ifill was a journalist; why has she become famous enough to be on a United States postage stamp?
2. There is more than one way to make your voice heard. Can you list some ways you can be a spokesperson?

Journaling:

What would you write about Harriet Tubman and what you are learning from this book that you would like to see published in the newspaper, or maybe on your blog?

Publish your writing:

Write a review of this book and share it. Thank you! This link is to Goggle https://g.page/r/CYTg0YMLzhTCEB0/review

Chapter 8

Trust Your Gut Feelings

I did what my conscience told me to do, and you can't fail if you do that.

— Anita Hill

A Christmas Letter

One year a few weeks before Christmas, I started having some troubling spirits about three of my brothers. I just felt they were in danger. I knew I needed to go get them out of Maryland soon. I couldn't wait until after Christmas. I had a friend that could write and send a letter to a man named Jacob Jackson. Jacob lived near my family back in Maryland. Now Jacob was a free colored man that could read and write. I knew that his mail was going to be read first by the mailman because every colored person was under suspicion for helping slaves escape.

So, I had my letter written in codes. Jacob had an adopted son named William Henry Jackson that lived in the North. I have a brother name William Henry, so I made sure my friend signed the letter with his name. I knew Jacob would understand. The letter started with a few lines of talk about the weather and asking about the crops. Then I had this put in: Read my letter to the old folks and give my love to them. Tell my brothers to be always watching unto prayer and when the good Old Ship Zion comes along, to be ready to step on board. See the "Old Ship Zion" was one of those songs they taught us, so, they didn't think much of us putting songs in our letters. But you see, William Henry didn't have a mother, father, or grandparents, nor did he have any brothers. The mailman felt something was not right, but he couldn't figure it out. He called in some other men to read it. None of them could figure it out. They called Jacob in to read the letter and asked him what it meant. Jacob read the letter. Then he balled it up and threw it down. Jacob said, "That couldn't be for me, I can't make head or tails of it." Hee-hee. Old Jacob got my message, and he went right away to tell my bothers to be ready because I am coming to get them soon. When I got there, I found out there were plans to sell off my bothers. I got there just in time.

Trust your Gut Feelings

Trust your gut feelings, use your problem-solving abilities, and be creative with your communication styles.

Harriet Tubman had a strong dependency on her intuitions. She used her knowledge of what she knew about how a letter to a friend would be handled. She got creative. The letter had a message that would be passed to the person it was intended for and not other readers.

Activities

Discussion questions:

Anita Faye Hill was born July 30, 1956. She is an American lawyer, educator and author.

1. Why is Anita Hill famous? What did her gut feeling tell her to do?
2. What do you think about her decision?

Journaling:

1. Write about any experiences you have had with a "gut feeling."
2. What did this experience teach you about your intuition?

Get creative:

1. Write a coded message that you know someone who the message is not intended for would not understand the message. (This could be a picture map, or a hidden item in the picture that would be hard to find, unless you had some knowledge about where to look.)

Chapter 9

Make Time for Quiet Time

"If I want to be alone, someplace I can write, I can read, I can pray, I can cry, I can do whatever I want - I go to the bathroom."

— Alicia Keys

My Prayer Closet

Well, I took care of my mama, daddy, and anyone else that found their way to my door with no place else to go. It seemed like there was always someone that didn't have nowhere else to go. I took in a couple of children, a blind woman, and some folks sick and near death. I always had a house full of people that depended on me to take care of them. My brother William Henry and his wife Catherine helped as much as they could. To support all of us, I raised pigs, chickens, grew apples and vegetables to sell, and for a while, I had a brick-making company with my husband, Nelson. Still, we could barely make ends meet. Sometimes in the winter, there was nothing to eat.

I remember one time, Mama was complaining about not having no food, no tea, and no tobacco for her pipe. I got so tired of hearing all the complaining, I had to escape. I went into my prayer closet. I had to get alone to talk to God. When I came out, I grabbed my basket and told my sister-in-law to put a big pot of water on the fire. When I get back, we're having stew. Well, I didn't have no money. I went to the market with faith. It was almost closing time. I first went to the meat market; I just stood there looking pitifully as a lost kitten at the nice meats. The butcher saw I was troubled and asked me if I had any money. When I said no, he said, "Tell you what, you can take this soup bone and when you get some money, come back and pay me."

I said, "Thank you, I surely will." I went on to the next stand, the vegetable stand, and the farmer gave me some potatoes and carrots. Do you know, when I got home my basket was full and we had a hardy beef stew. That's how it was, I had to depend on the Lord to take care of us, because there was never enough money.

Make Time for Quiet Time

Make time for quiet time. Put a pause between making a decision. Find ways to get away from challenges, daily tasks, or busyness. Refreshing your mind makes better thinking. Take some deep breaths. Harriet Tubman found a little spot in her house where she could be alone. After this withdrawal, she had her solution to the problem at hand. She came out ready to take action.

Activities

Discussion questions:

Alicia Keys, (Alicia Augello-Cookis), an American singer, songwriter, record producer, pianist, and actress. She was born on January 25, 1981, in New York City, she began playing the piano at a young age and showed early musical talent.

1. What is your favorite Alicia Keys song?
2. What do you like about the lyrics of this song?
3. How do they affect you?
4. How is Alicia helping others?

Research Alicia Keys' foundation, Keep A Child Alive https://www.keepachildalive.org/about-us/

Journaling:

1. How do you withdraw and take quiet time?
2. What do you know about meditation?

Try something new:

Visithttps://karolvbrown.com/theharriettubmanway/meditation/ for some beginner's meditation links. Try a few of the suggestions you find on these links.

Chapter 10

Bless Others

The success of every woman should be an inspiration to another.
We should raise each other up. Make sure you're courageous, be
strong, be extremely kind, and above all, be humble.

— Serena Williams

On the Route to a Better Life

When folks ask how many people, I brought up out of
slavery, my memory fails me. I know I made about eight trips before
I went to get Mama and Daddy. I guess by that time, I had brought
up about seventy other folks too. Some folks keep better count than
me because they wrote it down. Folks like Mr. William Still in
Philadelphia kept records of all the slaves that came through
Philadelphia. When Sarah Bradford was writing her book on me, she
took information on the number people who traveled to freedom
with me from Mr. Still and other Underground Stationmasters that I
visited. When she counted everyone from the records kept, she
figured it was about three hundred. I don't remember that many
people. She might have counted people I told how to leave Maryland
on their own. I do know it was over seventy people that traveled
with me. There are some trips back to the South that I'll never forget.
My first trip back was in December 1850. I went back to Baltimore
and brought away my niece and her two children, who had come up
from Cambridge in a boat. Her husband was a free man, and he
planned that trip. He pretended to help his master buy them at an
auction. Instead of delivering them to the new owner, he delivered
them to me in Baltimore.

I remember the trips to get all my four brothers free, three of
them on one trip on Christmas day. Then there was that trip when I
had about thirty-nine people with me. That was the time we had to
backtrack in the wood and hide in the swamp. Children, I tell you,

thirty-nine people was too big of a group for me. I didn't do that no more.

Now, I'll never forget that scary riverboat trip with Tilly. Tilly was about eighteen years old, in love, and brave. The man she wanted to marry had gone North and she was about to be married off by her master to someone else. She had decided she was leaving, and she was waiting for me when I got to Maryland.

That trip was planned to take a ferryboat to get to the free states. I had friends get our tickets and to write out some passes for us. When we gave our tickets to the ferryboat conductor, he asked for our travel papers giving us permission to be getting on this boat without our masters. We gave him the papers, but because me and Tilly couldn't read, we didn't know what the papers said. He told us to wait. The conductor went back into the building, and we sat waiting on the side of the river to get on the boat. We had no place to run to, so we had to act like we were supposed to be there. After everybody else was on the boat, he came back and gave us our traveling papers and our tickets. I was praying hard for the Lord to get me through that one.

Bless Others

Share your blessings and be dedicated to helping others. Love, compassion, community, and responsibility are valuable tools for taking actions.

Harriet Tubman went back to bring others up to a better life. There were about three thousand known conductors on the Underground Railroad. Some of those conductors were ex-slaves who could not enjoy freedom knowing those they left behind were suffering. Seek to help others achieve what you have, or more. Remember we are blessed to bless others.

Activities

Discussion questions:

Serena Jameka Williams was born September 26, 1981. She is an American former professional tennis player.

1. What does the Serena Williams Foundation do for others?
2. Who are the people; family members, teachers, and friends you can list that have blessed you by helping you live a good life?
3. What does it take for one person to help many other people?

Journaling:

1. Think about your passions, your concerns about your personal world. How can you be of service in a way that can help yourself and other people?
2. What kind of support would you need to take this action?
3. Who could you ask to assist you?

Make a detailed plan for one action you can take to be of service to someone. Include: what, when, how, who, why, and where.

Chapter 11

Love Nature

"You have to plan and cultivate good health. You have to commit to good health. You have to live good health because it comes from the inside out. It comes from what you bring to your life: positive, empowering thoughts, prayers and affirmations, uplifting company, and high-quality, life-giving foods. To have excellent health you must invest time and energy into the transformation of your Sacred Body Temple. And once you've acquired excellent health, you must maintain it vigilantly. That's the true divine challenge—one that you can and must meet."

— Queen Afua

When I was just a little girl, my daddy started teaching me about nature.

I loved being in the woods with Daddy. Where we lived in Maryland, there were swamps, wilderness, and rivers. Daddy showed me how to make bird calls and other sounds that the animals in the woods made. Then, I could use these sounds to send messages, or scare away some other creatures.

I could climb trees, slide on my belly quiet as a snake. When I needed to find something to eat in the woods, I knew which berries were good to eat. I could catch a rabbit and I could build a fire, too. Oh, and let me tell you, when Daddy told me about how to know when I am going North if I couldn't see the North Star, now that was a life saver. He taught me to rub my hands on the trees. The moss grows thicker on the north side of the trees.

Oh, I tell you, it could be a rough trip walking through the woods with bare feet. You ever seen a sweet gum tree? Well, I tell you, those trees dropped a thorny little seed pod that hurt so bad when you stepped on them with bare feet. Those seed pods were even harder when they dried up in the winter.

Now, in the summer, the swamps, woods, were green and it was easier to hide, but summer is not the season that I planned my trips to go back to Maryland.

Even though the winter was not the time of year most people would think of running away with no shoes and decent clothes for freezing weather, winter is when I planned my trips. Think about it. Look outside at supper time in the summer. What do you see? Plenty of daylight, and plenty of folks hanging around visiting. Now how does it look in the winter? It's darker earlier and folks are not outside so much in the winter. So, that was the time to get folks traveling in the darkness of a long night.

Another thing I knew about when I planned my trips: slaves didn't have to work on Sunday. So, I made sure that my party would meet up, out in the woods, or at a graveyard, where nobody would see them, on Saturday.

We could get a good head start before the masters even knew anyone was missing on Monday or Tuesday. Now, if I hadn't been around there growing up as a slave, I might not have known this was the schedule that I could plan around. I paid attention to what was going on around me. That helped me on all my travels.

Daddy worked in the woods for years and he knew about roots, flowers, and herbs that were good for medicine and taste good to eat. I learned about how to make root beer from the ginger roots. I didn't know the names of all the plants, but I learned fast which plants not to touch, because they would cause a rash or make you sick.

I knew the purple flowers were good for keeping us from getting sick. I used what he taught me about medicines when I was working as a nurse during the War. That's right, it was the herbs I found that I gave soldiers and freed slaves to help get well from the disease they call Dysentery.

After folks started traveling with me, they started making up stories about how good I was at being in the woods. I heard them say, "Moses can run as fast as a rabbit. She can climb a tree as fast as a raccoon. Moses can hear a patroller's dog bark ten miles away. And you should see her jump over a fence like a deer." Ha-ha. I don't know about all that. But I am thankful that I did know how to read signs of nature and to use what I knew to get my people free.

Love Nature

Take time to smell the roses, the daisies, and the trees. Appreciate what the rain does for the Earth. Learn to notice your surroundings.

Harriet Tubman, as did everyone during the time she was living, depended on the sun to shine to let them know it was morning. They looked at the changes in colors of the leaves on the trees to alert them to the time for planting and picking.

Nature was a part of everyone's life. Harriet was very in-tune to her surroundings, and she paid attention. She could have just disregarded what her father was teaching her. But she remembered and found this love of nature to be a big factor in her successful travels on the Underground Railroad.

Activities:

Discussion questions:

Queen Afua, (Helen Robinson) was born on August 22, 1953. She is a renowned holistic health practitioner, wellness coach, and an accomplished author, who has been a trailblazer in the green food's movement for over four decades.

1. What would you consider Self-Care?
2. What does holistic mean?
3. How much water are you drinking a day? Are you drinking the recommended amount?
4. Keep a food diary for 3 days, count the number of vegetables and fruits you ate each day. Do you need to make some changes in how you eat?

Journaling:

1. Look out your window. What do you see? Describe what is outside your window.

2. Is there anything new to your eyes? Are there things that change with the seasons?

Get creative:

Show us what nature looks like around you. Draw, paint, sing, dance, or write a story or poem. If you don't see much to talk about, use your imagination as to why nature is important.

Chapter 12

Love Your Community

The greatness of a community is most accurately measured by the compassionate actions of its members.

—Coretta Scott King

Steal Away

I remember, we colored folks had our own preachers, but we couldn't have church unless we had a white preacher sitting there watching and listening. He was to keep an eye on us and tell us what they wanted us to know out of the Bible. What they wanted our preacher to say is, it was God's will for colored folks to be slaves and them to be our owners. We all knew better than that. They allowed the colored preacher to tell us about the part when God freed slaves from Egypt and how Moses took his people to a land of milk and honey. I loved that story and I loved to hear about Jesus. What we held on to was how Jesus loves everybody and He came to save His people and that included us. I learned the stories about Jesus and the stories He told. Mama taught me always to hold steady onto Jesus and he would see me through this tough life. I learned I can talk to God anytime and I didn't have to talk aloud. I always talked to God every day, just like I am talking to you right now. I talked to Him, and I would ask Him to save me from slavery. You know, he talked back to me too.

I learned a lot from watching and listening to other people. Mama and Daddy taught me about what I needed to know to survive slavery, but I didn't just have my own family to learn from. All the colored folks around where I lived were like family. We had to be. You never know when your own sister, brother, father, and mother would be sold away, and you could be left with no family. So, you called all the women around "Sister" and the men were your "Brother."

Mama was "Mama" or "Auntie" to all the children around. We took care of each other as best we could. Although we attended the white church, we looked forward to our own services. On certain nights, we'd "Steal Away to Jesus." In other words, we tiptoed out to the camp meeting, an invisible church under the stars and the bright moon. Usually, it was near a creek where folks could fish. We had plenty of food out there in the woods. Folks brought sweet potatoes and corn to roast in the big fire. Sometimes there were roasted ducks and fried rabbits and steamed clams, crabs, and oysters fresh from the Chesapeake Bay. The fiddlers, old and young, would grab a corner and go to fiddling. There were always some banjo players strumming. Flames from the fire would be jumping to the beat, up ten feet high. Field hands and house workers blended their voices like a choir of songbirds. Someone would call out a part of the song, and we'd sing it back to him. It was truly soul singing because we meant those words that we sang to God; we really wanted Him to hear us.

Before the preaching, the men set up a wagon by the fire for the preacher to stand on so everybody could see. Then the preaching and the teaching would start. We would hear, as the preacher said, "a word from the Lord." Now that's when those stories we learned in church with the white man there changed a little. I found out all about Moses and the Israelites leaving Egypt was the same as God freeing my people and taking us out of slavery. We learned how Jesus was born to save all of us and that included us colored folks. After the Bible lessons, it was time for stories and the news that folks picked up from the white men talking to each other. When I was little, my grandmother Modesty was one of the old folks from Africa who told us stories about being free.

We heard all about the stories of freedom back in Africa and how colored people owned property and were kings and queens. Her stories made me know I had a right to my freedom. I heard about freedom in this country called Up North. Those stories also taught us how people used the North Star to guide them all the way to freedom.

I found out there were people that would help you run away from slavery if you found the tracks on that Underground Railroad. They said that the railroad tracks start in the South and take people to freedom Up North. But you have to find the right people at the train stations. My eyes got big listening to these stories. I would ask my daddy where I could find those tracks. Daddy said, "Minty I can't tell you. I'm afraid you would run off to try to find them." Well, he was right about that. I was all ears listening to those stories to see if I could figure out where to find those Underground Railroad tracks. I asked everybody who told the stories, and I got all kinds of answers, because people really didn't know what the Underground Railroad was or if it was real. Every time you heard those stories, they got more farfetched. Those were times I remember when we could get a good laugh. These times kept me going. It was our love for each other, and the bonds that I developed that let me know when I got my freedom, I had to go back for my family. All these people were my family.

Love Your Community

Develop positive relationships. Be supportive to others and accept support from others.

Harriet Tubman's extended family gave her love and support. Everyone needs someone that he or she can call family. This is why people join clubs, churches, and gangs and develop other relationships. People need supportive people. The support and love from family, friends, or a group of like-minded people provides many chances for growth.

Strong relationships make you stronger through hard times. Positive, loving relationships build character and a strong spirit. Avoid negative or unhelpful relationships; they can lead to destruction of your spirit. Your service to others is Love In Actions. The more Love In Actions that you practice, the more love will grow and the community you call yours will increase and become stronger. Each loving relationship develops more happiness, support, and a feeling of responsibility for each other.

Activities

Discussion questions:

Take some time to think about who you have around you in your home, neighborhood, school, and even larger communities. What kind of support do you need from others?

1. How do you find positive supporters?
2. Do you give support to others?

Journaling:

1. List some positive people that influence you. Explain what these people do that you like about them.
2. Describe what others do to support you.
3. What are ways that you can support other people?

Be curious and creative:

Coretta Scott King was born on April 27, 1927, and died on January 30, 2006. She was an American activist and the wife of Dr. Martin Luther King, Jr.

1. Find another quote from Mrs. Coretta Scott King to share with your classmates. Yolanda Renee King, born May 25, 2009, is the only grandchild of Dr. Martin Luther King Jr and Mrs. Coretta Scott King. Listen to her interview about her new book, Yolanda Renee King NPR January 15, 2024
2. "For all the elected leaders out there who are tweeting, posing and celebrating my grandfather, Dr. King, today my message to you is simple: Do not celebrate, legislate." Yolanda Renee King

3. Use your preferred artistic expression to share something that would be an example of one of Mrs. Coretta Scott King's quotes.

Karol V. Brown

Part Two

Self-Empowerment

"True power is living the realization that you are your own healer, hero, and leader."

—Jada Pinkett Smith

With self-love comes self-respect, self-determination, and self-empowerment. You can take charge of your destiny. If you don't believe that, review what I said about Harriet Tubman's childhood. My guess is that you have a much better chance than Minty did to become the woman that you dream you will be.

Dreams that you feel determined to reach are what inspire your goals. Goals are important. This is where you do the planning that leads to you realizing your dreams.

Parents often want to lead children in the direction they envision for them. It is important for children to have parents that have dreams for them. However, it is up to you to believe that there is no goal too big for you to achieve. This is self-empowerment: knowing and believing that you can do anything you set your mind to doing.

Figure 6 Young Harriet Tubman

Chapter 13

Envision a New World

This is a long, long, faraway goal, but 2036 I am running for office to be president of the United States. So, you can put that in your iCloud calendar.

— Amanda Gorman

Fly Away and Escape Dreams

Ever since I was hit in the head with that two-pound weight when I was about fifteen, I started having sleeping spells. That's when my dreams got to be more real to me. Sometimes I'd be working in the field, and all the sudden I'd fall asleep. When I wake up, folks tell me I was asleep, but it seems to me, I was awake and watching a story in front of me.

I called these my Escape Dreams. First, I would hear music playing. I say, "Y'all hear that music?" Nobody heard it but me. Then, I'd travel out of my body and I was flying up in the air with the birds, higher and higher. When I looked down, there were the rivers, the fields, and the treetops. It was beautiful. Then I'd come to the line separating the land of freedom from the land of slavery. Every time I'd try to cross over to freedom, on the other side were some white women in white dresses and they called out to me, saying "Run, run for your life." Then, I'd fall short of crossing the line and I'd wake up, still in slavery. Over the years, I had this dream over and over, and all the while, I believed I should be free. I could see a new world for me.

I had reasoned out in my mind that I had the right to one of two things: my liberty or death. If I couldn't have one, I'd have the other. I would fight for my liberty as long as my strength lasted.

Wasn't no man going to take me back to slavery alive. If the time came for me to go back, then I wanted the Lord to take me to be with Him. When I finally got free and met different people who worked on the Underground Railroad, some of those white women I saw in my dreams were the women I met up North. My dreams come true.

Envision a New World

Be brave and have a passionate vision for your life. Hold on to your dreams; know where you want to go. Know that with a sense of direction, your vision will come true.

In Harriet Tubman's time, it was unbelievable for a third-generation slave child to have any thoughts that freedom for herself was possible. The difference between Minty Ross and many other slaves that never tried to run away was courage. She wasn't afraid to dream big. She was not afraid to believe that she deserved to have a better life. It was her right. She wanted freedom so badly she could see it, feel it, and hear it. Later, she realized it.

Don't be afraid to dream the impossible. Nothing is impossible.

Activities

Discussion questions:

Amanda Gorman was born March 7, 1998, she is an American poet and activist.

1. Find some of her poems and recite one to the class. Discuss what she was saying in the poem.
2. What is an activist?
3. What do you want to be doing in the year 2036? Do journaling activities about dreams.

Journaling:

Review what you have written before about your dreams.

1. How have the stories of Harriet Tubman and the other leaders mentioned in this book influenced you and your dreams?

Visualize your dream in a dream or vision board:

What does your dream look like, sound like, and feel like?

Make a vision board. You can get creative and make a collage out of pictures from old magazines. Add quotes, pictures, or find pictures on the web to put into a document that you can print off when you are finished.

Use the sections as an outline of your dreams:

1. What is your dream?
2. What does it look like? Draw or write the description.
3. What will it take to get to this dream?
4. What are you doing now to prepare for the future?
5. Who will be with you when you reach your dreams?
6. How will you feel when you achieve your dream?

Keep a copy of this vision board, write it out on paper, and review twice daily.

Chapter 14

Dedicate Your Life to Your Passion

Passion is energy. Feel the power that comes from focusing on what excites you.

—Oprah Winfrey

I Have to Take Care of My People

When I crossed the line from the land of slavery into the land of freedom, it felt glorious. But I could hear the moans and groans of my people back in slavery. I said to myself, "I am free, and they deserve to be free too."

I prayed to God to send me back. He did and He protected me every step of the way. Time after time, I went back and thanks to the Lord, I got my family and about seventy other people out of slavery. Then the Lord said, "Harriet, now that you got your people free, you got to take care of them."

I took care of my mama, my daddy, and anyone else that found their way to my door.

When the Civil War started, I knew that meant freedom for all my people, and I wanted to go and help. The army needed me to work in South Carolina. Now my parents and all these other people depended on me to support them. But I felt I had to go help out in the war. I left my parents with my brother, his wife, and my friends that agreed to take care of them.

Part of my duties was looking after the people who were slaves who ran away from their masters and came to the Union Army for help. The army didn't know what to do with all these colored folks. They were not really free, and they couldn't fight in the army. They call these people contraband. They had nothing. Some barely had clothes on their backs. On the plantations, their masters taught them to do one thing, work in the rice fields. When the Union Army moved in, all the white people ran away and the work in the fields stopped. When the work stopped, so did the food supply for the colored people. Some of these poor souls were sick.

Just like back at home, I felt I had to take care of these people. I worked in the colored hospital and did the best I could to lighten the burden on the government. At the same time, I did all I could to teach my new people how to respect themselves by earning their own living.

Dedicate Your Life to Your Passion

Use love to motivate you to show that you are responsible. Have compassion. Pray for others. Make sacrifices. Help people build self-esteem and self-respect.

When Harriet Tubman committed her life to helping others, she kept focused on this goal, which was to take care of the needs of others. She did not stop. She was challenged, she may have grown weary, and she was not healthy herself. Yet, she accepted the responsibility that comes with leadership and her plan was to fulfill her commitment as a lifelong duty. If you have a commitment to empower others, start by encouraging them. Stay focused on that goal.

Activities

Discussion question:

Oprah Winfrey was born January 29, 1954, and is an American media proprietor, talk show host, actress, producer, and philanthropist.

1.	What are some ways Oprah Winfrey has shared her passion of talking and working with people that will change lives?

Journaling:

1.	List what you love doing. This is an activity that makes you feel good, useful, happy, and proud. Something you want to be able to always have as a part of your life. This could be your passion.
2.	What does it take to be truly dedicated to a cause?

Get creative:

Tell a story. Who do you know who is an example of dedication to his or her passion? If you can, interview this person. If you can't do an interview, talk to other people or research this person on the internet. Write one page about them and prepare to tell their story to your classmates.

Chapter 15

Listen and Learn

My mother said I must always be intolerant of ignorance but understanding of illiteracy. That some people, unable to go to school, were more educated and more intelligent than college professors.

—Maya Angelou

I Can't Read, but I Can Learn

Now I never did learn to read or write, but I did learn to listen and to learn from what other folks knew and talked about. Learning from others helped me understand this world better. What I learned help me make my own decisions about what was wrong and right. Even though most of my white friends were well educated and I was not, they learned from me too.

After I got free, I spent a good part of the year traveling around to the abolitionists' meetings in Pennsylvania, New Jersey, New York, and Massachusetts. I made new friends. One of my friends was Franklin B. Sanborn; he was a writer for a newspaper. Mr. Sanborn took me to the homes of his friends. I was introduced to well-known people; writers, businessmen, bankers, and politicians, they were all abolitionists. They spoke about ways to end slavery that I never even thought of. Some of the families were very rich and I stayed in their big, beautiful homes. I was there as their guest, and I ate at their tables, and I slept in their guest rooms, not in servant rooms. They lived very different lives from me, but that didn't stop us from being friends. I had some good discussions with some folks, smart folks like Mr. Amos Bronson Alcott, he was a teacher, his daughter, Louisa May Alcott was a writer too. Little Women is the name of one of her books.

Mr. Horace Mann was a Massachusetts US House Representative. Mr. Ralph Waldo Emerson, another writer, was also in on the discussions around Boston. Frederick Douglass would be at most of these meetings, and he was the only one besides me who knew what it was like to be a slave. I was sitting around folks that ran the newspapers, wrote books, taught in colleges, but I couldn't read to learn what they taught. I didn't have to, I just listened, and I learned about how the government worked, how they made their money, and how they could change folks' minds about slavery by writing in newspapers.

When I told them my story, they would write it in the paper to let other folks know how slavery was bad for the country. In our discussions, we talked about how it could take a war to change this country. They talked and I listened about who should be the president and how the right person in that office could end slavery. As I listened, I started to understand how I really did have a right to be free. It was in the paper called the Declaration of Independence. In that paper written long before I was born, it says "All men are created equal." My friend John Brown let me know that I should consider myself as equal as any man. He even called me General Tubman. I said to all these smart people who taught me about the Constitution and Declaration of Independence, "If you all really believe in these things written long ago, then you all have to continue the struggle and be willing to fight to end slavery." As Frederick always said, "If there is no struggle, there is no progress. If that means war, then we need to get ready for war." Before meeting Frederick and me, those white folks had only read about slavery, or saw some actors play like slaves. Some of them had never even been in the South. Frederick and I compared life in the North with life in the South for a colored person.

We told them about growing up as a slave. I taught them the dances we did in the camp meetings back in Maryland and had those folks dancing and singing "Go Down, Moses" and "Steal Away to Jesus." They learned by listening to us, and we helped them understand why what they did to help was important. I learned enough from my experiences and from listening to them to tell them what I thought. Now that they knew more about what slavery is like, I knew if they were truly good people, they couldn't stop their writing and speaking until there was no more slavery in this country. I was proud that I got to tell my story my way and teach these smart folks something they couldn't learn in school. We got to know, trust, and understand each other just by talking and listening to each other.

Listen and Learn

Develop your listening skills. Look to increase the diversity and cultural exchange in your group of friends. This leads to more equality, respect, and informed decisions. Good leaders have great listening skills.

Harriet Tubman was not formally educated, but she was smart. She knew how to be an active listener. Education is powerful and life changing. Listening and hearing are the same, but different. Hearing does not necessarily mean understanding what you hear. When you are listening, there is a process of interpretation in order to understand the message. Active listening involves questioning what you heard, getting more information, and being able to respond with an exchange of ideas.

Activities

Discussion question:

Maya Angelou was born on April 4, 1928 and died on May 28, 2014. She was an American writer, poet, singer, and actor.

1. Dr. Maya Angelou was a great communicator. Find one of her poems. Review it and be able to explain what you think she was saying in the poem. You might even read it aloud to your group.

Journaling:

Define the following terms that are part of good listening skills.

- Eye contact
- Visualization
- Feedback
- Clarification
- Nonverbal
- Questioning
- Nonjudgmental
- Empathize
- Don't interrupt
- Attentiveness

Practice with a listening game:

Go on the internet and find a listening game and teach it to your classmates.

Chapter 16

Practice Communication Skills

*What does music mean to me? I don't think I would really be much
without it, without it coming through me. It's my means of
communication, my means of growth, my means of transportation
from one point in my life to another.*

— Erykah Badu

Talking Without Talking

Now us colored folks couldn't talk about heading off in the middle of the night for a camp meeting. Oh no, we had to use the grapevine. We had the same language that the white people had, but we had to learn to give it a double meaning. When it came time for passing on secret information, we found ways to talk that didn't sound like talking. Most of the time, the message was in the songs we sang. A song about the River Jordan became a song about crossing over the river that took you to freedom in the North. See what I mean? We took the words from the songs and the Bible scripture the white man taught us and used that as code words for places and other meanings that we wanted to talk about to each other. Take the song "Steal Away to Jesus." Sometimes when folks sang this song, they were talking about running away, but if the song passed from person to person, you knew it had a different meaning. The white folks taught us this song, but they thought we couldn't always remember the words. They figured if we sang it a little different, they didn't care. They didn't know that we could get all the details we needed in a few verses.

When "Steal Away" passed from the woods where the men cleared the trees to the field where people were working all day, up to the big house and back down to the slave quarters, that was a message. We all knew what, when, and where we were to meet on Sunday night.

Through this process, I learned how to communicate in a way that only the folks I wanted to get the message got the message. When it came to leading people away from slavery, we needed to talk without talking.

Practice Communication Skills

Your ability to communicate well can make the difference in the outcome you seek. Learn to use verbal and nonverbal forms of communication. Be creative.

Harriet Tubman was also able to communicate with people outside of her own family group. She learned new words from her educated friends. She was able to communicate in two cultures. There are differences in people's culture and education that influences their ability to understand each other. Nobody follows someone that he or she can't understand. A leader must have a special way of connecting.

Love is the secret behind the "special way." It means one cares enough to find the right words or an alternate means of sharing one's thoughts to be understood. Sometimes you cannot convey in words the message you want to relay. Remember the saying, "actions speak louder than words." If you need to express love, show it in your actions. "Love In Actions."

Just like in a text message and emojis, friends have their own shorthand and special language. This is the same as what Harriet used. Songs were her "text messages."

Activities

Discussion questions:

Erica Abi Wright she was born February 26, 1971. She is known professionally as Erykah Badu. She is an American singer and songwriter.

1. Do you know Erykah Badu's style of singing? Select one of her songs and share what she is communicating in her lyrics.
2. What are some special words, gestures, or expressions you use that only a few people in your close group of friends or in business setting understand?

Journaling:

Write the definitions to these terms that are examples of good communication skills.

- Listening
- Nonverbal communication
- Clarity
- Friendliness
- Confidence
- Empathy
- Open-mindedness
- Respect

Learn new languages:

Find out how to say these phrases in a different language. Practice saying the phrases, record your voice, or video yourself. Identify what language you are speaking. Share with your classmates.

- I love you
- Thank you
- Hello beautiful
- Let's be friends
- I appreciate you

Chapter 17

Study People with Influence

*Part of why history is so important in my life is because it brings
you an awareness that everything isn't new. It gives context to
what's happening right now. History is cyclical but circumstances
and technology change. So, when social justice topics come up,
they're not new. They're just being covered more. We have more
ways to record it now.*

— *Yara Shahidi*

General Tubman

I remember the first time I met John Brown. Frederick
Douglass brought him to meet me in St. Catharines, which is in
Ontario, Canada. He walked in, gave me a salute, and said, "The
first I see is General Tubman, the second is General Tubman, and
the third is General Tubman."

That made me smile. I couldn't believe that this white man
I'd heard about that hated slavery as much as me came to talk to me.
Not only that, but the great John Brown also called me General
Tubman. Well, that was something to remember. John Brown took
me to abolitionist meetings at the home of Wendell Phillips (a rich
lawyer) in Boston. He introduced me as one of the best and bravest
persons on this continent. He said, "General Tubman can lead an
army as well as any military man that ever lived." He even called
me a "brave man." To have a white man put me up as an equal to
any man, black or white, almost brought me to tears.

After John Brown started taking me to these meetings, I went
back time and time again, sometimes without him. When I spoke to
those white men, they listened to me like the soldiers listened to a
general. They respected me, and I respected them.

I found out later that these meetings were to help John Brown plan his raid at Harpers Ferry. John Brown wanted me to bring as many-colored men as I could to help him fight for our freedom. I was doing all I could to bring men together to fight under John Brown, but my health wasn't too good around that time.

When he and his men made their attack, I was at home sick. After the Harpers Ferry raid where John got caught and killed, I knew I had to keep on talking to powerful people and fighting against slavery by speaking out and getting ready to go to war.

John Brown had introduced me to some men called the Secret Six. They were all abolitionists, but to be the most helpful, they had to keep their own feelings about slavery from the public. I can tell you their names now, since all that was years ago. They were John Brown's good friend Mr. George Luther Stearns, a powerful businessman; a doctor, Dr. Samuel Gridley Howe; two preachers, Rev. Thomas Wentworth Higginson and Rev. Theodore Parker; and Franklin Sanborn, who was a professor. We mostly met at the home of a very rich man, Mr. Gerrit Smith. I got to listen in and give my own thoughts on some very secret discussions.

There were lots of words they said that I didn't understand. So, I asked plenty of questions and they explained things to me. Gerrit Smith said words like, "My rights all spring from an infinitely nobler source, from the favor and grace of God. Truth and mercy require the exertion, never the suppression of man's noble rights and powers. Our political and constitutional rights, so called, are but the natural and inherent rights of man, asserted, carried out, and secured by modes of human contrivance." (BrainyQuote)

After he explained all that in simple words, I liked what he said. In my own words, it is just what the Lord told me years ago; I had the right to my freedom or death.

Study People with Influence

Respect earns respect; politics is people and power. Know the names of the powerful people and study their politics.

Harriet Tubman did what she was compassionate about. When you show your compassion, people respect what you do. Others with similar beliefs and causes will be drawn to you. People who work together have power.

Synergy is a great word. It means working together to get greater results than working alone. This is what politics is about, people using their power by working together to influence the government affairs. Politics is at all levels of life: home, school, church, community, city, state, national, and international. Start where you will feel the most impact; in your home, school, and community. Getting involved in a cause that you are enthusiastic about can make a difference. Servant leaders start by serving others in some way, later as they find the need to do more, they find themselves as a leader who continues to serve.

Activities

Discussion questions:

Yara Sayeh Shahidi born February 10, 2000 is an American actress and producer.

1. What has Yara Shahidi been doing outside of acting?
2. What has she seemed to learn from studying history?
3. What are you learning from Harriet Tubman and the women quoted in this book?

Journaling:

1. What issues or causes concern you?

2.   How can you work with others to strengthen your power to make change on what you are concerned about?

3.   Look up the word synergy and make a list of ways you have observed this concept in action.

Give the Best Test:

Find the names and contact information for your local, state, and US representatives and senators. Make a note on how they stand on the issues that concern you. See if they pass Mr. Greenleaf's "Best Test."

(See the Best Test in the section, The Tubman Way to Legendary Servant Leadership.)

- Mayor
- City council members
- School board
- State representatives and senators
- US representatives and senators

Chapter 18

Be a Woman with Passion and Dedication

Any time women come together with a collective intention, it's a powerful thing. Whether it's sitting down making a quilt, in a kitchen preparing a meal, in a club reading the same book, or around the table playing cards, or planning a birthday party, when women come together with a collective intention, magic happens.

—Phylicia Rashad

Strong Women

When I got up North, I met many men abolitionists giving some great speeches about ending slavery, but there were some powerful women too. One of them was Sojourner Truth. She was a big woman who'd been a slave in New York. Like me, she worked as hard as a man. She always felt we women were as worthy of rights as the men.

I heard about her speaking up one time at the National Women's Rights Convention in Ohio. A man tried to say why women couldn't have rights. He was trying to say women were helpless and men had to help women into carriages and over mud puddles. Sojourner stood up, made her way to the front of the room, looked that man in the eyes, and said, "Nobody every helped me into a carriage or over mud puddles. Ain't I am woman?"

She was right when she said, "We do as much, we eat as much, and we want as much as a man." She said that man who said, "Women can't have rights because Jesus wasn't a woman." Sojourner looked that man in the eyes and said, "Mister, where your Jesus come from? I tell you where He came from—God and a woman. Man had nothing to do with Him. If that first woman God ever made could turn this world upside down all by herself, I know all these women here today can turn it right side up again. Now that

71

they are asking to do it, you men better let them." You know that brought the women to their feet.

I remember talking to Sojourner about what life would be for colored women after we were all free. What we found out was that after the war was over and we were all free, it was time to fight some more. We had to fight for the right to vote, the right to go where we wanted to go, and sit where we wanted to sit.

I met Susan B. Anthony at her home in Rochester, New York. She helped me with some of my passengers headed to Canada. Susan B. Anthony and Elizabeth Cady Stanton were some strong women, and they had a dream that women in this country would vote. They marched in the streets and spoke at rallies. I marched with them sometimes. Once someone asked me if I really believed women should be able to vote. I looked at him and said, "I suffered enough to believe it."

I remember one time when I was in Rochester, Miss Anthony took me to a rally with her. I remember coming in the room and sitting down, but I must have fallen to sleep. The next thing I knew somebody was calling my name and shaking me. I wasn't sure what they wanted me to say, but I told them I had worked on the Underground Railroad and "my train never jumped the track, and I never lost a single passenger." I guess they liked that because they cheered.

Marching with Miss Anthony was all about getting the right to vote for women, but colored women had more problems than voting. Colored women decided we needed our own meetings and groups. We knew we were the ones that had to take care of our children. We wanted to make sure our children got an education. We organized to help poor folks with food, clothes, and to do all that we could for our people.

I was right there with Josephine Ruffin, Mary Church Terrell, Ida Bell Wells-Barnett, and Frances E. W. Harper when we formed the National Association of Colored Women. Our motto is "Lifting As We Climb."

Yes, I've been fighting for freedom and rights for a long time and taking care of folks the best, I could. Now that I am too old to get out there and march myself, I want to keep the women encouraged.

I told them that the Lord is with you, so you women stay strong and keep on working to make the world better for our children and families.

Be A Woman with Passion and Dedication

Be a woman who seeks strong women for comradeship, support, joint efforts, advocacy, and as mentors.

Harriet Tubman was a woman of action and she sought out other women to work toward improving life in America for everyone. Women are strong and when dedicated to a cause, they are unstoppable. Women can and should work toward supporting each other. Older, more mature women are important in the development of self-esteem and leadership in younger women. Appreciate the loving spirit of strong women in your life, be encouraging, and learn from them.

Activities

Discussion questions:

Phylicia Rashad was born on June 19, 1948. She is an American actress, singer, and stage director.

1.   Phylicia Rashad is a woman with many talents and accomplishments. What are some of the awards she has won? Why do you think she has accomplished so much in her life?

2. Can you name some women in your life that you feel are strong and determined?
3. What are some of the traits these women demonstrate that make them great leaders?

Journaling:

1. What are some of these traits that you share with these great leaders?
2. Visit our website www.karolvbrown.com/women and girls to learn about some women's organizations that you may want to follow on social media, support, and maybe join.

Chapter 19

Find Mentors

Your environment doesn't define you. I don't have a lot of money, but I can help train people and I can talk to people. We can all be mentors to the next generation.

—Jacqueline "Jackie" Joyner-Kersee

I Learned from My Friends

Up North, colored folks were teaching the Northern white folks about slavery; how it was wrong. Abolitionists were the folks who knew that slavery was wrong and were willing to do something to end it.

I had many colored and white friends that wrote about ending slavery. Frederick Douglass was a great speaker and he and I would travel and speak at abolitionist meetings. Frederick published a newspaper called the North Star, and he wrote several books. I learned a lot from Frederick. William Still (a colored man) in Pennsylvania wrote for a newspaper called the Herald of the Local Vigilance Committee. In New York City, my friends Mr. David Ruggles (a colored man) and Mr. Oliver Johnson (a white man) worked together to write the National Anti-Slavery Standard. Then there was Mr. William Lloyd Garrison (a white man), the editor of The Liberator. Things he said in his paper really got some people stirred up to act.

Mr. Garrison wrote; "That which is not just, is not law. The apathy of the people is enough to make every statue leap from its pedestal and hasten the resurrection of the dead. Wherever there is a human being, I see God-given rights inherent in that being; whatever may be the sex or complexion. You cannot possibly have a broader basis for government than that which includes all the people, with all their rights in their hands, and with an equal power to maintain their rights." (Brainy Quote)

Because I could not read, I had to have him explain what he wrote. When he finished, I said, "Oh, I agree, all God's children have a right to freedom."

Some folks that escaped slavery only talked to folks like themselves, other ex-slaves who never learned to read or write. Some of them felt they shouldn't try to have friends that had an education and seemed to be different from them.

I ask some folks, "How're you going to learn something new if you only talk to folks who only know what you know?" I learned a lot from my smart friends. They taught me more than I would have ever learned as a slave. All that I learned helped me understand this world better.

My teachers were the folks that I watched, listened to, and talked with that knew some things that I didn't know. I know the importance of education, whether you learned it from a book, or if you learn from other people.

Find Mentors

Seek out knowledge from other people. Learn from your own experiences and other people's experiences.

Harriet Tubman took advantage of opportunities to learn from other people. She never learned to read or write, but this didn't stop her from increasing her knowledge. Don't be afraid to associate with people with more education or people who are different than you. Most people are willing to share their knowledge with others. It is up to those wanting to learn to find someone with the information you would like to know and to listen to them.

Activities

Discussion questions:

Jacqueline "Jackie" Joyner-Kersee was born on March 3, 1962. She is an American, retired Olympic athlete who competed in the women's heptathlon.

1. Why would someone who wants to compete in the Olympics want to talk to Jackie Joyner-Kersee?
2. What are the roles of a mentor and a mentee?

Journaling:

1. What do you want to learn more about that you could learn from someone with experience in that field?
2. Who do you know that knows something about this topic?

Reach out:

Search social media sites to find someone that you would like to talk to about your interest. Be brave and send them an email. Explain that you are interested in their field and ask for an appointment for a brief phone call. Prepare your questions before the call. Listen more than talk. Don't forget to say thank you and send a thank you note, email, or card.

Chapter 20

Realize On-the-Job Training

When I was a kid growing up, I always thought I would be a journalist, and I thought, you know, I'd cover stories about other people, and we're always taught never to make the story about yourself.

—Tamron Hall

From the Time You Can, to the Time You Can't

Well, children, y'all know I had a hard life. But we all did. We worked hard as slaves. We worked from the time you can to the time you can't. In other words, if the sun is up and you can see your hand in front of your face, it is time to go to work. Work stopped when you couldn't see to work no more.

I knew that if I didn't do my work right, I was going to get whipped. If I didn't do my work fast enough, I got whipped. To avoid whippings, I worked hard and fast on all my chores, except housework. I knew how to do housework, but I hated it. I did just enough not to be whipped. After a while, they figured I wasn't good at housework, and they put me outside to work.

Like I told you before, I was just about six years old when my master sent me to work for Miss Susan. While I was working for her, I had to be up at sunrise to have the table set for breakfast, clean the house, and hold that baby anytime she didn't need to feed him. Then at night, I rocked the baby to sleep and stayed up all night making sure he didn't wake up crying. I learned to take little catnaps instead of really sleeping. That came in handy when I was traveling on the Underground Railroad because I had to keep watch for the patroller's day and night.

I worked in the woods and in wheat and cornfields. For years, I chopped about a half-a-cord of wood a day. I followed the oxen behind the plow, loaded and unloaded logs, and carried heavy loads in and out of barns. I was working as hard as any grown man was. I got strong out there in the field and the woods.

Because I learned early in life to work hard, I didn't have problems finding work when I got to Philadelphia. I knew how to do about anything. I could cook, clean house, do laundry, and sew. I worked in the hotels and in homes.

Do you know the biggest difference in working hard as a slave and as a free person? I am sure you're thinking that the answer is that I got paid. Being paid was one big difference. But, the best part was that I could choose who I would work for when I was free. There were good employers and bad ones. When I didn't like the way I was treated or I was not learning anything new on a job, I left and found another job. Now that is freedom.

Realize On-the-Job Training

Learn from all experiences and keep a positive attitude. Stay optimistic and appreciate that every day is an opportunity to learn something new. Never give up your self-respect, which is self-love. Harriet Tubman's life lessons started early.

Sometimes life lessons are hard and even cruel. You might not realize at the time, but each day is a learning experience that is a resource for developing your personal goals and leadership style. Those lessons include learning the difference between the right way to treat people and the wrong way.

Activities

Discussion questions:

Tamron Hall was born September 16, 1970. She is an American broadcast journalist, television talk show host and author.

1. How many different positions did Tamron Hall have before she was able to have her own TV show?
2. What do you think she learned from the other shows that has helped her have a successful talk show of her own?

Get creative:

Answer the questions. Share your information in a format of your choice: picture, story, collage, poem, song, or another creative way.

1. What are your fields of interest (for example, entertainment, education, sports, business, or health)?
2. What education is needed for your selected position?
3. Where can you get the training or education you need for this career?
4. What skills are needed for this career?
5. What are your plans for the next five years to prepare for this dream future?

Chapter 21

Keep the Faith

Seeds of faith are always within us; sometimes it takes a crisis to nourish and encourage their growth.

—Susan L. Taylor

God Led the Way Across the River

I always talked to God, and He talked to me just like I'm talking to you. He would tell me to trust Him. I remember one time I had three stout men traveling back up North with me. We were moving along at a good pace. It was early in March, a cold, snowy, bone-chilling night. All of a sudden, my heart went to pounding, it like to jump out of my chest. That was how the Lord got my attention to listen to him. God said, "Harriet, stop! Get off this road!"

I didn't walk another step forward. I said, "Come on, brothers, we got to go this way." I headed off the trail into the woods. I hadn't traveled this deep in the woods before, so I didn't know what we would find. We came to a river. I looked up and down that riverbank and I didn't see a boat, or a bridge. What I did see was the ice forming on the top of the water, and I knew we had to wade across it. I went in first; the men stayed back waiting to see what was going to happen to me.

The water was the coldest I had ever been in, to this day. The water kept getting higher and higher, up to my armpits, then my neck. I went to praying: "Oh, God, you have brought me through six troubles, please don't leave me on the seventh." The water didn't go no higher, I made it across, and the men folk followed. We were freezing and shivering, and our teeth were chattering, but we kept going until we came to another stream. We had to cross that one too. We were wet, freezing, tired, and my bad tooth was aching, but we went down the road until we came to a cabin.

Now I didn't know if we would find friends or foes, but the Lord told me to trust Him. When I knocked on the door, I was happy to see that some colored folks lived there. They were kind enough to take us in for the night. Oh, children, I was so grateful. I wanted to pay them, but I didn't have any money. The next morning, we got nice breakfast and dry clothes. The wife said, "Miss Harriet, these are some nice woolen underwear, I ain't never seen some so nice." I said, "Baby you can keep them." I paid them with my underwear. Do you know what I found out when we went on to the next station? I found out that up about a mile from where we got off the road, the owner of the three men with me was up there waiting. If we had taken even a few more steps, they would have heard us and they would have captured us. I just say every night, "Lord, where would I be if You ain't been on my side?"

Keep the Faith

Have faith, never give up, and follow your feelings, it could be God talking to you.

Harriet Tubman knew God on a personal level. She believed he would take care of her, and she did not hesitate to follow God's directions. Faith kept her going, and it was her faith that allowed her to overcome obstacles and the negative comments from those with less faith.

Often, you are the only one that holds on to the faith that you can accomplish your goals. Hold on, you might have to change your route, but don't let fear stop you from reaching your goals.

Activities

Discussion question:

Susan Taylor was born on January 23, 1946, and is an American editor, writer, and journalist.

1.   Susan Taylor was the editor-in-chief for Essence magazine. But that was not her first job with Essence. What was her first job and her educational background when she joined Essence?

Journaling:

How do you define faith?

1.   Look up some definitions of faith.
2.   List some that you can identify with and keep in your mind at all times.

Listening to songs:

1.   Visit my website to hear this song that Harriet Tubman sings, "If It Had Not Been for the Lord On My Side", and see my song list for Self-love and Women Empowerment at: www.karolvbrown.com

Figure 7 <u>*www.karolvbrown.com/songs*</u>

Songs and Playlist

If It Had Not Been for the Lord on My Side

> If it had not been for the Lord on my side, tell me
> Where would I be, I want to know now,
> Where would I be
> You know He kept my enemies away,
> He let the sunshine through the cloudy day
> He rocked me in the cradle of His arms when He
> Knew I had been battered and scorned
> So, if it had not been for the Lord on my side
> Tell me where would I be, I want to know now,
> Where would I be?

2. Share a song that you can sing when you need to strengthen your faith. List the words of the song, and if you have a sample of the song, play it for your classmates.

Chapter 22

Keep a Sense of Humor

Smiling is definitely one of the best beauty remedies. If you have a good sense of humor and a good approach to life, that's beautiful.

—Rashida Jones

The Chickens Chase

Life can be rough, but it's good to be able to laugh too. I remember one time; I was on a trip back to near where I grew up in Maryland. I knew it was a good chance I could run into one of my old masters, so I needed to be in disguise. One of my best disguises was as an old woman. I knew most white men in the South hardly looked at an old colored woman, so all I needed to do was to put on an old bonnet, get me a stick for a cane, and walk bent over and I was hidden in plain view. I thought about how I would get away if I got too close and someone did really look at me. I had a plan.

I got me two live chickens. I tied their legs together loosely with a rope and started down the road past the Bucktown store. Just like I thought, here comes one of my old masters, headed my way. Well, I just made a little tug on the rope to loosen up the knot and the chickens were loose. They were a cackling, and I was acting like I was trying my best to catch them. I was really just chasing them through the street. I'm sure it was a funny sight to that white man looking at this old granny chasing some chickens. Just like I thought, he didn't try to help me. He just let me pass on by through town, chasing chickens. He was just a foot away from the woman he wanted for stealing his property as he called us. He was laughing aloud at me and I was laughing silently at him. Hee-hee. Folks love to hear me tell that story.

Keep Sense of Humor

Keep your sense of humor. Stress can block the creativity and logical thinking. Being able to make people laugh is a universal tool for making a positive connection. Humor breaks the ice, personalizes an encounter, and builds relationships. Finding some humor in life is a powerful leadership skill. Harriet Tubman used stories, songs, or jokes to decrease the stress and anxiety of her passengers.

Activities

Discussion questions:

Rashida Jones was born on February 25, 1976. She is an American actor, director, writer, and producer.

1. Rashida Jones has acted in several comedies. What kind of personality traits do you think it takes to act in comedy programs?
2. Rashida is biracial. What are some of the challenges she might have had growing up?
3. What are ways that humor can be a tool for coping with life's challenges?

Journaling:

1. Who makes you laugh?
2. How do you feel after a good laugh?
3. How can you learn through humor?

Learn to tell a joke:

1. Find a joke you can share with your classmates.
2. Make sure your joke does not offend anyone.
3. Practice the joke with your family.
4. Make a video of yourself telling the joke.

5.   Share your joke.

Chapter 23

Keep On Going

Decide what you want. Declare it to the world. See yourself winning. And remember that if you are persistent as well as patient, you can get whatever you seek.

— *Misty Copeland*

You've Got to Keep on Going

When I was traveling on the Underground Railroad nobody traveling with me ever got caught and I never lost anybody along the way neither.

Before we took off, I'd say, "I'll get you safely to freedom, but it ain't going to be no easy trip. You're going to be cold, scared, and hungry, but if you leave with me, there's no turning back." I was serious about that.

One time, I had a party of about eight people. We'd been on the road about four days, gone through a half dozen stations on the Underground Railroad. I had a man with me that had some sore feet. Well, I felt bad for him, he was like so many folks and didn't have any shoes. He said, "Moses (that's what they called me), I can't make it. Go ahead and leave me. I can't walk another step. I can rest and then go back to the plantation." I reminded him what I said: "There's no turning back." We tried to wrap up his feet. He kept saying, "I can't walk another step, and I'm going back." That is when I had to pull out my pistol.

That's right; I carried a pistol with me on every trip. I said, "Look here, I can't let you go back. If you're too weak-minded to walk to freedom on some sore feet, it won't take much whipping from your master when you get back for you to tell all you know about the stations on the Underground Railroad. Those people who help us are our friends. They gave us food, clothing, hiding places, and rides to the next station. I ain't going to let one coward put the lives of so many people at risk. "You either get up and walk or you'll die right here." When he knew I was serious about shooting him, boy I tell you, you never seen someone jump up and move so fast! Once he was free, he thanked me and said he was sorry. I never had to shoot nobody. I just had to let them know I was determined to get them to a better life. It was worth scaring them a little. Hee-hee.

Keep On Going

Know where you want to go. Understand the obstacles you may meet and be determined to keep on going. Your goals are the motivation for your actions. Advocacy requires dedication, commitment, giving your trust, and keeping your word.

Harriet Tubman was a leader who set her goals high. She risked her life many times to help those who wanted to be free. She knew that to achieve her goals, she needed help from others. She gave them her trust and she would not jeopardize that trusting relationship. Her sincerity in her mission made all necessary means of escape acceptable to her. This may seem a little extreme and possibly questionable in terms of her ethics. However, it was her style, and it is our personal style that makes us human. There are no perfect humans. Remember, she felt she was on a mission for God. Like Harriet, trust God and never doubt that you will succeed with every goal you set. "Let go and let God." Also, practice being nonviolent.

Activities

Discussion questions:

Misty Danielle Copeland was born September 10, 1982. She is an American ballet dancer for American Ballet Theatre.

1. What does it take to become the first African American woman to be promoted to principal dancer at the American Ballet Theatre?
2. What are you determined to achieve in your life?

Journaling:

1. What do you know that you do better than anything else?
2. If you wanted to have a career doing this you love, what would it take for you to reach a professional level at what you do? In other words, how can you make money doing what you love to do?

Visualize your goal:

Design a medal or trophy for yourself when you reach your goal. Take a picture of yourself with your medal and keep it in your journal or on your wall where you can see it. Feel proud of yourself and grateful for your achievements.

Chapter 24

Say Thank You

"Thank you" is the best prayer that anyone could say. I say that one a lot. Thank you expresses extreme gratitude, humility, understanding.

—*Alice Walker*

I Am So Grateful

Children, I am so grateful. I am grateful to God for bringing me through. I always knew He was with me every step of the way. See, I talked to Him every day, just like I am talking to you now. He let me know when I needed to listen. My heart would start to pound, and I knew He was telling me He had something to say. I always felt like a pillar of clouds protected me by day and a pillar of fire protected me by night. I never went nowhere He didn't tell me to go. God sent me food when we didn't have nothing to eat. I'd go into my prayer closet and ask for His help when we didn't have no food or money. Whenever folks showed up at my door with food or clothes or money, I thanked them, and I thanked God because He knew I needed help and He sent it every time.

I'm grateful for my freedom. When I got free, I felt like I was in heaven it felt so glorious. I knew that freedom was worth fighting for and I decided I needed to do something to help others. God told me what to do, go back to free my people. I was grateful that He chose me. Many people have thanked me for their freedom. I tell them to thank God.

You know, when the people who traveled to freedom with me let me know they were thankful, it made me feel good inside. I thanked God for that good feeling too.

Say Thank You

Express your gratefulness to God and be modest. Harriet Tubman provided examples of how she communicated with God. She would get to a place to be alone and where she could pray and hear God talking back to her.

She never took credit for doing anything herself. She felt any help that came to her, came from God. She trusted him and thanked him for all he did. She listened to his voice in different ways. This is her intuition, the fast heartbeats, and a small voice in the head telling her which way to go.

Everyone has some intuition. Don't ignore it. Be grateful and look and listen to God speaking to you. Remember to thank him for what you have, what he has done for you, and what he is doing for you every day. Also, be thankful today what is coming tomorrow as if it has already come.

God works through people. Don't miss an opportunity to thank the people in your life who have sacrificed, supported, and in any way been good to you. People remember other people by the way people show their appreciation. Be remembered as someone that is grateful.

Activities

Discussion question:

Alice Walker was born on February 9, 1944. She is an American author and activist.

Alice Walker wrote The Color Purple. This book was made into a movie and a Broadway play.

Research her life and discuss what she had to overcome to become a successful writer.

Journaling:

1. Write down ten people or things for which you are thankful.
2. Make a habit of listing ten things you are grateful for every day.
3. What can you do to show that you appreciate people in your life?

Say thank you:

Write a little thank-you note, or draw a picture, sing a song, or just say thank you to the people on your list who have sacrificed for you and that you are grateful for.

Chapter 25

Make Your Money Work for You

Excuse me while I save, invest, and build wealth.

— Stephanie Lahart

I Worked and Saved Every Penny

I have worked hard in my life. I had a good use for every penny I earned, even when I was a slave. I learned that if I worked for hire, that's when my master would get paid for me working for someone else. If I worked extra hours after the master got his money, I could keep the overpay for myself. That's all I needed to know.

I was up before sunrise to work the fields, clean the barn, haul the wheat to the mill, and chop wood. Before the day was out, I cut about a half-a-cord of wood a day. That hard work paid off. I saved enough to buy myself a pair of oxen worth forty dollars. With my own oxen, I could work a plot of land and grow more vegetables. I sold my own vegetables, and that money was mine to keep. I planned to buy my freedom. But that never happened. I ended up running away before I had enough money to buy my freedom.

When I got up North, I already knew how to live with just bare necessities. I worked to save my money for my trips back to get my people.

I had many different jobs. I worked in Pennsylvania, New Jersey, and New York. I could get jobs really easy down in Cape May, New Jersey. Lots of rich folks came to the beaches in the summer and there was plenty of work in the hotels.

My best way of making money was as a storyteller. I would go to the abolitionist meetings in rich people's homes, and they would invite their rich friends. I would tell stories about being a slave in Maryland. People would make donations to my cause of rescuing my people. I kept every penny I made, and when the winter came, I was ready to head back to Maryland to get my people. I put my money to work to make my trips on the Underground Railroad successful.

Make Your Money Work for You

Financial goals demand some sacrifices. Save your money for important expenses. Learn to budget your money.

Harriet Tubman was able to use the little money she had to support her mission. Learn to be thrifty and do with less today in order to do more tomorrow. Learning to share your stories can pay off more than you know. You might talk for a living, or the way you make a living requires you to talk and being able to tell stories is a great skill to develop. Either way, learn how to manage your money. There will be many ways the money can help you with your goals.

Activities

Discussion question:

Stephanie Lahart is an author of several books and a motivational speaker. Check out Stepanie's book: "Teens Matter Most: A Powerful, Straightforward Guide for Teens. Your life has purpose, and you are important!" Share what you learned.

1. What do people in your family say about money?
2. What conversations have you heard about investing and building wealth?

Journaling:

1. What are ways for you to make money that you can save?
2. What are some purchases you can delay or adjust to decrease spending and save more?

Research activities

1. Research these terms:
   a. 50-20-30 budget rule
   b. Interest rate
   c. Compound interest
   d. Return on investment
   e. Stocks
   f. Bonds
2. If you have a job and are paid $50.00 a week, using the 50-20-30 budget rule, how much should you be saving each week?
3. Where would you put your money to make it grow and keep it safe?
4. Open up an account that you find is best for your money. Start saving.

Part Three
Become a Legendary Servant Leader

Education is for improving the lives of others and for leaving your community and world better than you found it.
—Marian Wright Edelman

Legendary Leader

Love extends beyond one's family. The care of those without families: orphans, elderly in nursing homes, and people suffering from mental illness all need the support and love from others in the community. Love is the key for a strong, healthy community. Harriet Tubman's sense of responsibility for her community is where her service and leadership passion developed. This is where she had power.

What is power? Power is the ability to do something or act in a particular way, especially as an inherent mental or physical quality.

Any one person can influence others through their leadership.

History shares many stories of powerful leaders. Not all are ones we want to emulate. But there are many, like Harriet Tubman, that are examples of how love, service, goals, and determination can be the influence that leaves a great legacy. I want girls to dream big and believe they have superpowers.

Parents, teachers, and mentors are set to help you. Harriet Tubman did not work alone, she was part of the Underground Railroad society. Through this network of people, she was able to navigate and achieve a 100 percent success rate for rescuing people from slavery.

A leader with a 100 percent success rate is unheard of. But, she did it in her own Harriet Tubman way.

Her leadership skills included critical thinking, communication, creativity, collaboration, and knowledge of nature that she learned throughout her childhood. She was a visionary; she could see herself in a better place than slavery. Her visions were real to her. What she saw in her thoughts became her reality. She also had faith, compassion, and determination that contributed to her success.

Araminta Ross faced just able every obstacle one could have against her. She had to overcome the cruelty of slavery, poverty, illiteracy, racism, physical and mental abuse, and a devastating disability. It was unlikely that this little slave girl, Araminta, would be known by anyone outside her extended family. However, she became the legendary leader we know and honor over one hundred years after her death.

Harriet Tubman is honored in books, art, music, movies, dozens of schools, museums, institutions, and on postage stamps. She received 118,328 votes from the American public to be the first woman on the United States paper currency, the twenty-dollar bill https://www.womenon20s.org/campaign.

A pretty good ending to the story of Araminta Ross, a little black girl with the superpower of LOVE.

Mark March 10 on your calendar as Harriet Tubman Day. Celebrate her life and continue to teach this legacy for generations to come.
http://www.harriettubman.com/day.html

Chapter 26

Volunteer to Serve

"Without community service, we would not have a strong quality of life. It's important to the person who serves as well as the recipient. It's the way in which we ourselves grow and develop.

— Dorothy Height

Nurse, Scout, and Spy

When the Civil War started, I knew it meant freedom for all my people. I decided to join up to do whatever I could do to help. I talked to my friends in Massachusetts where there was a group training-colored men to fight. The 54th Massachusetts Volunteer Infantry Regiment was going to be ready when President Lincoln gave the word. Before they would let us fight, we all volunteered to do other jobs, just to help out the government as much as we could. When the Union Army took Port Royal in South Carolina, all the white slave owners fled and left the slaves behind with no food and no way to care for themselves.

There was a plan to send teachers to South Carolina to help teach the ex-slaves how to read, write, and teach job skills that they needed to start new lives. John Andrew, the governor of Massachusetts, got me some papers to go down to work under General Hunter. My job was to help teach sewing and cooking and to care for the sick colored folks in the hospitals.

When I got to South Carolina, I learned General Hunter knew all about my many trips to the South without being caught. That showed him that I knew how to get in and out behind the enemy line. He said I could get information from the slaves that no white man could ever get. He asked me to be a scout and a spy.

I was willing to do whatever the government asked me to do to help end slavery. I worked long, hard hours, just as I did all my life. I didn't mind, because helping to make a new free world for my People was important work. I worked three years for the government. It was hard for me because I never got any pay for my service and my family back home needed money. But, I did my part to help all my people get their freedom, and that was more important than the money.

Volunteer to Serve

Transferable skills are useful in all types of service to others. Harriet Tubman used the skills she developed in one area in many ways. Whenever you are learning by doing, these skills are useful in all that you do. When you volunteer, the services you provide are important to those that are receiving your support. Nothing you do for others is a waste of time. Your payment may not be in dollars, but you will gain benefits through volunteering.

Activities

Discussion questions:

Dorothy Irene Height March 24, 1912 – April 20, 2010 was an African-American civil rights and women's rights activist.

1. Dorothy Irene Height was the president of the National Council of Negro Women for 40 years. What does this organization do?
2. How would volunteering for an organization in your community help you progress toward your goals?
3. Marian Wright Edelman was born June 6, 1939. She is an American activist for civil rights and children's rights. She is the founder for the Children's Defense Fund. What does the Children's Defense Fund organization do?

Journaling:

What can you do for an hour or two a week to help someone? Keep records of your volunteering time, your manager's contact information, and your volunteer job description. These volunteer jobs can be added to your resume.

Get started in service:

Take the steps to start serving at home, school, or in your community. Do something for someone else.

Chapter 27

Use the Powerful Tool of Networking

We learned about gratitude and humility—that so many people had a hand in our success, from the teachers who inspired us to the janitors who kept our school clean and we were taught to value everyone's contribution and treat everyone with respect.

—Michelle Obama

The Underground Railroad Was About People

The Underground Railroad was not a train on a real track; it was all about people. It was all kinds of people working together, colored folks, white folks, and Indians too. We used those coded words like stations, stationmasters, safe houses, and conductors. I was a conductor. All the folks working on the Underground Railroad risked their own freedom by helping slaves. If it were not for this network of people, I don't know where I would be today. It was a secret network, and they were very organized.

Some people like my friend Mr. William Still of Pennsylvania kept written records of the events in order to help escaped slaves find their family who came up before them.

Another one of my friends on the Underground Railroad was Mr. Thomas Garrett. Mr. Garrett was a Quaker, and he was one of the bravest, kindest men I ever met.

He spent forty years helping folks escape to freedom through his home in Wilmington, Delaware.

One time I needed money to buy supplies for the trips back and forth in the South. As always, I asked the Lord to send me what I needed. Well, the Lord told me to go to Thomas Garrett for the money. I knew Mr. Garrett wasn't a rich man. He was always good about giving me food, shelter, and shoes for everybody in my groups of passengers, but I didn't get much money from him. This time, when I got to his house and told him I needed money, he said in his Quaker way of talking, "Harriet, why do thee think I have any money I can give thee?" I said, "God told me you did." Mr. Garrett said, "Well Harriet has your God ever deceived thee?" I said, "No sir, never." He said, "Well how much did he tell thee to ask for?" I said, "About $23.00."

He looked surprised, not because I was asking, but because just a few days before, Eliza Wigham over in Scotland sent him a letter. Way over in Scotland, folks had heard about me and wanted to help. In the letter was five pounds of sterling. In American money that is about $24.00. Thank you, Jesus!

Reference Letters

When Sarah Bradford sent letters to some of my friends, they wrote letters to her about me. They wrote some nice words. It's nice when you can find someone to say something good about you.

Letter from Hon. Gerrit Smith (Bradford, 1869):

Peterboro, June 13, 1868.

My Dear Madame: I am happy to learn that you are to speak to the public of Mrs. Harriet Tubman. Of the remarkable events of her life, I have no personal knowledge, but of the truth of them as she describes them, I have no doubt. I have often listened to her, in her visits to my family, and I am confident that she is not only truthful, but that she has a rare discernment, and a deep and sublime philanthropy.

With great respect your friend,
Gerrit Smith (Bradford, 1869)

Karol V. Brown

Letter from Wendell Phillips, JUNE 16, 1868:

DEAR MADAME: The last time I ever saw John Brown was under my own roof, as he brought Harriet Tubman to me, saying: "Mr. Phillips, I bring you one of the best and bravest persons on this continent—General Tubman, as we call her." He then went on to recount her labors and sacrifices in behalf of her race. After that, Harriet spent some time in Boston, earning the confidence and admiration of all those who were working for freedom. With their aid she went to the South more than once, returning always with a squad of self-emancipated men, women, and children, for whom her marvelous skill had opened the way of escape. After the war broke out, she was sent with endorsements from Governor Andrew and his friends to South Carolina, where in the service of the Nation she rendered most important and efficient aid to our army. In my opinion there are few captains, perhaps few colonels, who have done more for the loyal cause since the war began, and few men who did before that time more for the colored race, than our fearless and most sagacious friend, Harriet.

Faithfully yours,
Wendell Phillips. (Bradford, 1869)

Appointment as Nurse

SIR: I have the honor to inform you that the Medical Director Department of Virginia has been instructed to appoint Harriet Tubman nurse or matron at the Colored Hospital, Fort Monroe, VA. Very respectfully, your obdt. servant, V. K. Barnes, Surgeon-General. (Bradford, 1869)

Use the Powerful Tool of Networking

Networking is being social and building positive relationships. Harriet Tubman had friends that introduced her to their friends. These connections provided opportunities she would have never found by herself. Respectful relationships build strong networks. If you ever need a reference, the relationships you have built will benefit you greatly. Remember never to burn your bridges. In other words, don't leave a relationship with bad feelings. You never know when you need to call on someone from your past to say something good for you.

Activities

Discussion questions:

Michelle Obama was born on January 17, 1964. She is an American attorney and author who served as the 44th First Lady of the United States from 2009 to 2017.

1. Michelle Obama has many great quotes. To read more of her words of wisdom that relate to self-empowerment, faith, withdrawal, and more, visit https://karolvbrown.com/the-harriet-tubman-way/michelle-obama-quotes/ (Use QR from *How To Use this Book* section)
2. Share one of Michelle Obama's quotes that is meaningful to you.
3. Think about what Michelle Obama said about all the people who have helped you. Share your thoughts.

Journaling:

1. Who can you ask to write a letter of reference for you?
2. What characteristics do you demonstrate in your relationships with people that make it easy to find someone to say something nice about you?

Research activity:

Research the concept of six degrees of separation between people.

Map it out:

See Diagram 1.

Make a drawing starting with a circle in the middle of the page. This represents you. At the edge of the paper draw another circle. This is your goal.

Now, between you and your goal, make five circles and lines to connect them. In each circle, write in the name of someone who can help you connect to your goal.

Networking is making connections with people who can help you reach your goal.

Diagram 1: Six degrees of separation worksheet

Diagram 1.

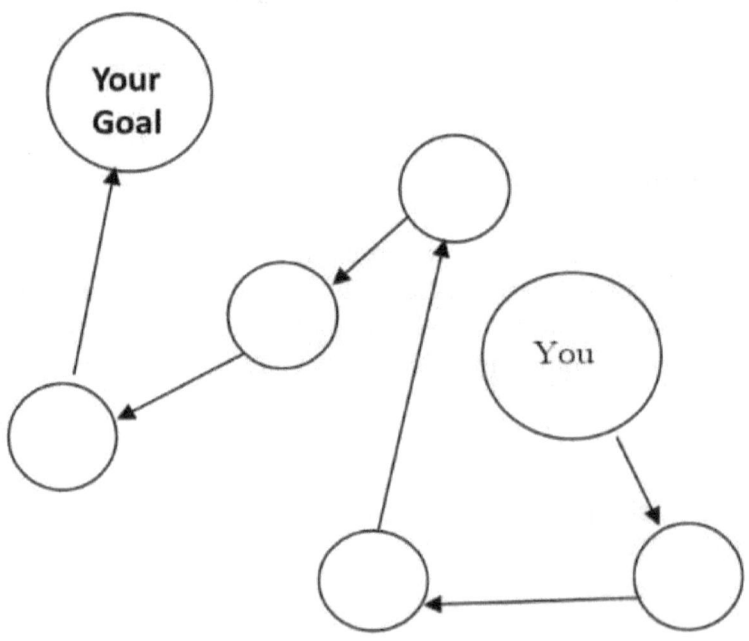

Chapter 28

Have a Plan B

Life is full of surprises and serendipity. Being open to unexpected turns in the road is an important part of success. If you try to plan every step, you may miss those wonderful twists and turns. Just find your next adventure do it well, enjoy it-and then, not now, think about what comes next.

— Condoleezza Rice

The Third Trip for Rachel

My last trip back to Maryland was just before the war. My friends were scared for me to go back again. The rewards were high on my head, and the slave owners in Maryland were spending big money to hire bounty hunters. My sister Rachel was the reason I had to go back this one last time. I had been back for Rachel two trips before. Every time I came, there was a problem.

She had two children and she refused to leave them behind. On the first try, one child was hired out to another plantation. Rachel's owner had just lost some other slaves and was not letting anybody leave to visit family. The second time, Rachel was sick and couldn't make the trip.

Most of my trips were in the winter. I never knew what kind of weather I would run into back in Maryland. This time I walked right into a snowstorm. I had sent word on ahead that I was on my way back to get Rachel and I was not going to leave without her this time. I waited in my meeting place out in the woods about two miles from where Rachel stayed. She didn't come, but the snow and the wind did come.

I prayed and prayed, but I didn't dare leave this place and have her come looking for me and I be gone. So, I found me a spot behind a big tree to block the wind and I stayed there all night. It was freezing, but the Lord was with me. He protected me and my toes didn't even get frostbite.

After the storm passed, I made my way to where Rachel stayed. That's when I found out she had died just a few weeks before I got back. Nobody knew where I could find her children. I was heartbroken my last sister was gone. I didn't want to waste a trip, so I asked if there was anyone else wanting to go back North with me. A man with his family (his wife and three children, one just a baby) asked to go. I agreed to take them. It was a hard trip, one of the hardest I had. We had to make changes in our route three or four times. The baby would cry, and I had to find some roots to give her to put her to sleep. The snow and ice made it hard to walk and the poor children would be so tired. It took about three weeks to get them to the North, but, we made it. Well, y'all, I went back for three and brought out five. Sometimes, even when things don't go as you plan it, it can come out all right.

Have a Plan B

As a visionary, you should know that everything does not always go as planned. Be prepared to change your course but continue on your path to your goal.

Being compassionate, resourceful, and flexible are traits of a great leader. Harriet Tubman's love and determination kept her going back for her sister. She did not grow cold and heartless with the heartbreak of losing her sister. Instead, she transferred the compassion to others.

Many things can factor into the journey toward a goal. Don't be so focused or narrow-minded that only one route to your goal will be acceptable. You should always have an alternate route to your goal or be ready to make up a new plan on the spot.

Activities

Discussion questions:

Condoleezza Rice born November 14, 1954 is an American diplomat and political scientist. She previously served as the 66th United States Secretary Of State and as the 19th U.S. national security advisor. Rice was the first female African-American secretary of state and the first woman to serve as national security advisor.

1. What kind of decisions did Condoleezza Rice have to make when things changed as the Secretary of State?
2. Discuss what kind of challenges Condoleezza had been an African American woman in one of the highest leadership positions in the country if she did not have a solution to a big problem.
3. How do you react when there is a change in your plans?

Journaling:

What can you do a little differently to see how it feels to change your routine?

Try something new:

1. Take a different route to work, school, or to a friend's house.

Notice what you see different.

2. Did you learn something new? Write about it.

Chapter 29

Take the Responsibility to Teach Others

If we do not lift up women and families, everyone will fall short.

— *Kamala Harris*

William Henry and Catherine

Y'all know, I couldn't just walk up to folks on the farms and in the houses where they worked and sing, "Go Down, Moses" to let them know I was here to take them up North. We had to plan this out. I didn't always know how many was going back with me. I didn't know where they worked or what would be the best way for them to get away from the plantations. I had to teach folks how to plan their own escape from the plantation. Once they did that, then they could meet up with me.

My brother William Henry was in love with a girl named Catherine. He wanted to marry her, but her master wouldn't allow it. When I sent word to William Henry that I was coming for him, he sent word back that he wouldn't leave without Catherine. Neither he nor I could go to where she stayed to get her. So, I told them what could work, and they figured out how to do it.

William Henry took all the money he had saved and went to a tailor and bought a man's dress suit. He tells the story of how the tailor wondered why he was getting such a small suit. He made up a story about his master's nephew was coming to town and it was a surprise gift from his master. When the time had come to get ready, he walked over past where Catherine lived and threw the suit of clothes over the garden fence of Catherine's master's house. Catherine went to the foot of the garden, dressed herself in the suit of men's clothes, and walked away. When the master realized Catherine was missing, he ordered all the girls in the household to start looking for her.

The only person the girls saw was this handsome well-dressed colored man in the garden. They had never seen him before. They stared at him and he acted like they weren't even there. They watched him and forgot all about Catherine until "he" walked down the road out of sight. Well, you should have seen the grin on my brother's face when Catherine got to the meeting place. A few weeks later, they were free, married, and living in Canada.

Take the Responsibility to Teach Others

Be caring and empower others. Harriet Tubman knew she could not be everywhere and do everything her people needed. She did know that these people were smart, and if given instructions, they could do what they needed to do for themselves. Being able to empower someone is to give them the power in the way of education or motivation to do something for themselves. This gift keeps on giving.

Activities

Discussion questions:

Kamala Devi Harris was born October 20, 1964, she is an American politician and attorney who is the 49th and incumbent Vice President of the United States under President Joe Biden. She is the first female vice president and the highest-ranking female official in U.S. history, as well as the first African-American and first Asian-American vice president.

1.   Research some ways that Vice President Kamala Harris has helped women and families.

Journaling:

1. What do you know that you can teach someone else to do?
2. Write down how you do what you can teach.

    a. What is the lesson you are teaching?

    b. What is the goal that you want those you are teaching to achieve?

    c. What materials are needed for your class?

    d. How do you explain new concepts?

    e. Write out each step from start to finish.

    f. How will you evaluate if your lesson was learned?

Start Teaching:

Offer to give someone the directions you have outlined in your lesson plan.

Chapter 30

Build Diverse Teams

When I bought the [WNBA] team, I saw that no one really cared about them. Like the locker facilities that these young women have to work in-they weren't right. I want to give them the best locker room facilities and show them they're valued-because if you show them value, they're going to perform better. And this goes for all women, not just basketball players.

— Sheila Johnson

The Best Team Around

Because colored men and women couldn't fight in the war, I worked as a scout and a spy for the Union Army. I was in command of a team of scouts who helped in the planning of the movement of the Union soldiers.

The best scouts and river pilots in South Carolina were on my team. I knew that the best folks to help me around South Carolina were folks who lived there. The men that worked with me were local people, and they knew every inch of that area. We could talk to the colored folks on those big rice and tobacco plantations and find out what they knew about the rebels, particularly where they kept their supplies and where they hid their weapons.

After President Lincoln signed the Emancipation Proclamation, ending slavery in the Confederate states, he let colored soldiers fight in the war. When General Hunter asked me to lead several gunboats of colored soldiers up the Combahee River near Beauford to attack the rebels, I asked him if he would appoint Colonel James Montgomery as our commander. I met him when I was going to planning meetings to help John Brown. General Hunter agreed to appoint Colonel Montgomery.

Our mission was to destroy the rebels' torpedoes, railroads, bridges, and to cut off their supplies. My main riverboat pilot was Mr. Walter Plowden, who was the best in the country. Mr. Plowden brought with him some pilots who knew the channels of the rivers in this area like the backs of their hands. Now, you won't hear the names of my brave team anywhere else in the history books because these were colored men who didn't get no medals for what they did for the army and the navy. But, they are heroes just the same and they deserve some credit. On my team of scouts and pilots with Mr. Plowden were Mr. Peter Burns, Mr. Mott Blake, Mr. Sandy Selters, Mr. Solomon Gregory, Mr. Isaac Hayward, Mr. Gabriel Cohen, Mr. George Chisholm, Mr. Charles Simmons, and Mr. Samuel Hayward.

Early in the morning on June 3, 1863, we loaded three hundred colored soldiers in three gunboats and quietly sailed up the crooked and narrow Combahee River. We attacked them before they knew what happened. We weakened the rebels along that river by bringing away food, weapons, supplies, and almost eight hundred slaves without the loss of a single life on our part. Of these almost eight hundred free colored folks, nearly all the able-bodied men joined the army. Now that's what I call teamwork.

I didn't know it, but I heard I made some history. This raid was the first raid in this United States planned and successfully carried out by a woman—me, Harriet Tubman. I have to say it was the work of my great team that made it possible.

Build Diverse Teams

Teambuilding involves diversity, recognition and appreciation, shared decision making, and recruitment of skillful people with different backgrounds. Each person brings a unique perspective to the discussion. Listen to them.

As skillful as Harriet Tubman was, she could not do everything by herself. Teams help leaders reach their goals. The strength of a team is diversity. When you're able to work with people with different skill sets and from different cultures, you get better results. Great leaders know the importance of diversity on teams.

Activities

Discussion questions:

Sheila Crump Johnson was born January 25, 1949. She is an American businesswoman, co-founder of BET, CEO of Salamander Hotels and Resorts, and the first billionaire African-American woman. Sheila Johnson is team president, managing partner, and governor of the WNBA's Washington Mystics.

1. How did Sheila Johnson make her WNBA team play better by changing their locker rooms?
2. Why do you think their locker rooms were not well kept before Sheila Johnson took over?

Explain your choice.

Journaling:

1. Do you have a project or goal for which you need to have a team of people to help you be successful?
2. What makes the team you selected the best team?
3. What do you bring to the team that can make it a stronger team?

Describe Your Superpowers on teams:

Write a paragraph describing the strengths, talents and superpowers you bring to a team.

Chapter 31

Realize the Goals with Others

If Your Dream Only Includes You, It Is Too Small

— Ava Duvernay

Include Others in Your Success

I grew up as a slave and then when I was about twenty-four years old, I married John Tubman. When I was about twenty-nine, my old master died. He left his widow with slaves, but no money. I heard that she was going to sell two of my brothers and me to the chain gang in the Deep South. I said, "No! I ain't going." I told my brothers "We've got to go now." I didn't tell my husband or my parents because they would try to stop me. My brothers and I started out together, but they got scared thinking about what would happen if we got caught. I can't blame them. We all had seen the whippings of those caught after running away. They dragged me back, but I had made up my mind to be free.

The next night, I took off alone. I had met a white woman in town who told me if I ever needed help to come to her. I made my way to her house. She gave me some food and she said, "Follow the river, it flows North. Take these two notes and give it to the man at the next station."

Then it was up to me. Through the thick dark woods, walking at night and hiding in the day, all I knew was to watch the North Star, follow the river, and stay out of sight. It was just the North Star and me. I prayed for Jesus to walk with me.

One morning, even though I was tired, cold, hungry, and looking for somewhere to hide, I looked up at the sunrise. There was something special about that sun that came up like gold from behind the trees. I could feel it warming me up deep down in my soul. I tell you, it was the most beautiful sunrise I've ever seen.

It filled the sky with colors from deep dark brown, golden brown, to orange, and then to the blinding bright golden yellow. When the sun was up, I could see where I was. I had walked past these large, white, four-sided tablets, spaced a few miles apart. I thought they were headstones, but they were something quite different. On one side, there was a picture of a crown and a shield, and there were stripes from the top running down to the bottom. I found out later that these stones marked the Mason-Dixon Line. This line separated Maryland, the land of slavery, from Delaware and Pennsylvania, the land of freedom.

I was free at last! It felt so glorious I had to look at my hands. I turned them over on both sides to see if I was still the same person now that I was free. I felt like I had flown with the eagles all the way to heaven out of my body and into the body of an angel. The weariness, hunger, and coldness left me.

Oh, freedom! Sweet freedom! I was jumping and screaming, and shouting, "Thank you, Jesus!" I laughed and I cried, first tears of joy, and then sadness. I realized I was free, but I was a stranger in a strange land. Everybody I knew was left in Maryland. And my husband John, even though he was free in Maryland, he wasn't free in his mind. He didn't know what real freedom was like. He couldn't know it down there in that land where he had to carry papers to show white men, he was free—that ain't freedom! He didn't even know how to think of living a better life. I was in the North feeling like a new person in this freedom that none of my family knew about. I was all alone.

I remember a story about a man who went to jail for twenty-five years. In jail, he lived day by day and held on to the thought of being free and going home to see his family. Every day was one day closer. Every day when he finished another day in jail, he pretended he was home. He could see his mother's face; hear his sister's laugh when he made a silly face at her. He pretended in the morning when he got up that it was his father's deep voice telling him to get his work done.

Then after twenty-five long years, he was free and went home. But, his family wasn't there waiting for him. Everyone he knew was all gone, and gone so long that the people living there didn't even recognize his family name. Even the house where he lived was gone. It was as if he left one jail just to go to another lonely jail cell.

I was like that man, all alone, and I said to myself and to God, "I'm going to go back and bring my people to this free land." Well, the Lord heard my prayers and he sent me back. I got Mama, Daddy, and all my brothers and many of my community of folks I loved free before the war. I didn't have to tell them how to feel. They all felt the change that came with freedom. They were new people. Free to live a better life. Seeing my people happy made me so happy.

Realize the Goal with Others

Value your relationships. Let love and compassion be your motivation for success. Blessings are to be shared.

Harriet Tubman felt that freedom without someone to share it with will not bring lasting joy. Your family and friends are important to your success. You may reach the goal, but that is not the real source of happiness. Being with people you love and who love you is the source of the joy. God gives us people because we need each other. God blesses us to be blessings to others.

Activities

Discussion questions:

Ava Marie DuVernay was born August 24, 1972. She is an American filmmaker.

1. Which prestigious award was Ava DuVernay the first African American woman to win?
2. What does it take to become a film director? What kind of skills do you need to develop?

Journaling:

1. Visualize your dreams. Who do you have included in your plan?
2. How will you share your blessings?

Get creative:

Get your camera and take a selfie of you being happy and successful at achieving your goals. Take pictures or find pictures you have saved of the people you want to share what you are blessed with as a successful person. Make a picture collage and remember how blessed you are with the support of those you love and who love you. One day this picture will be reality.

Chapter 32

Build Trust Through Sacrifice

Power means happiness; power means hard work and sacrifice.

— Beyonce Knowles

I Made New People My People

When the War started, the government sent me to work with my folks—the colored people they called contraband. But, in South Carolina, they were not my people. They didn't know nothing about me. They laughed when they heard me talk; said I sounded more like the Yankees than I did to how they talked. And, I didn't know what they were saying when they tried to talk to me. They didn't trust me.

When I got to South Carolina, the government gave me $200.00 for my personal supplies. I decided to give up my rations and my cabin and move to where the other colored people lived.

I built a laundry with the money. I taught the women how to sew and wash the soldiers' uniforms. During the day, I worked at the hospital while the women worked the laundry cleaning the soldiers' uniforms.

Every night in my quarters I had some women helping me cook. We baked about fifty fruit and sweet potato pies and some loaves of gingerbread, and we brewed up two or three barrels of root beer. The next day while I worked in the hospital, the women sold what we made. I paid them, and for the first time in their lives they earned money and learned how to keep earning money. They were so proud of themselves. We were businesswomen supporting our families.

Soon we learned to trust each other. We worked together. The women talked to me, and I talked to the officers in charge to let them know their concerns. It didn't take long for these folks to become my folks.

Build Trust Through Sacrifice

Relationships are built on trust. Listen to understand and empathize with others to build trust. When people trust you, you are able to be influential and a leader they want to follow.

Harriet Tubman's love for all people and her willingness to serve meant that she had to earn the trust of the people she wanted to help.

Service to others may require sacrifices. Accept people for who they are and help them become their best selves.

Activities

Discussion questions:

Beyoncé Giselle Knowles-Carter was born September 4, 1981. She is an American singer, songwriter and businesswoman.

1. Beyoncé has been performing professionally since she was very young. Name some of the sacrifices she had to make in her life.
2. How influential can a famous person be to young people?
3. Are there positive issues and negative aspects of being influenced by someone famous?

Journaling:

1. When you're faced with the same or a similar situation as Harriet Tubman in this story, will you be willing to sacrifice finances and/or comfort in order to earn respect and connect with people?
2. Who has sacrificed for you?

Karol V. Brown

3. What will you give up for someone you love?
4. What if you loved your community, what can you do to show Love in Actions?
5. How do you show people that you are trustworthy?

Chapter 33

Show Love In Actions Everywhere You Go

Love, I find, is like singing. Everybody can do enough to satisfy themselves, though it may not impress the neighbors as being very much.

— Zora Neale Hurston

Just Passing Through Troy, New York

Most folks think I only had to battle for freedom in the South or during the War. Well, let me tell you about the day I had my own little war up here in the North.

I was on my way from Auburn to Boston to attend an anti-slavery meeting. I took the train, and I thought I would stop on the way to visit my cousin in Troy, New York. Before I could get out of the train station, I heard that the US Commissioners were trying to send a man back into slavery. I wasn't about to stand still and let that happen.

The man's name was Charles Nalle. If you saw him, you would have seen that he was just as white as his half-brother who was trying to take him back to be his slave. I found out where they had him, and I made my way there.

I put on a red bonnet, borrowed a cane, bent over, and this old granny walked slowly past a dozen white men into the courtroom. I got inside where they were holding Nalle, and I got over to the window. I told all the colored folks to get all their friends in the center of town, to keep watch on me in the window, and when I gave the cue, they were to yell, "Fire!"

When the officers started out the door with Nalle, I turned to look down on the crowd from the window, gave them the signal and the fire bells starting ringing. The crowd got bigger and excited. Just as they were coming down the stairs with Nalle, I grabbed hold of him around his neck and I was not going to let go. Nalle was handcuffed and the officers tried to get me off him. They clubbed me, clubbed him, and pulled one way on both of us while the crowd pulled the other way. It went on for what seemed like an hour. I lost my shoes; got my clothes torn to rags. Poor Nalle was beat about unconscious and his wrists were all bloody. But I held on. I said, "Drag us out, drag him to the river, and drown him! But don't let them have him!" They tugged and pulled and knocked us to the ground. While we were down out of sight, I took off my bonnet and tied it on Nalle's head. From then on, the commissioner's men couldn't see his white head standing out in the crowd of black heads. Finally, my folks got control and dragged us to the ferry, and they put him on it to get him out of town. I knew that wasn't the end of it. The commissioner had men waiting for Nalle on the other side of the river and they took him off the boat and to jail. Do you think I was finished? Oh, no! Hundreds of us got on the next ferry. I got the folks together on the other side and found where they took Nalle. We had to break down a door. Some men were shot. A man was hacked with an ax. I got some women to charge the door with me and we went in and pulled Nalle out. There was a wagon waiting to rush him out of town to safety. I guess you know that I didn't get to visit my cousin. I had to get out of that town. When it comes to talking about fighting for your freedom, I surely know what that's all about. I know you have to keep fighting to hold on to your freedom and the freedom of other people, too.

Show Love In Actions Everywhere You Go

Advocating for others means to take actions and stand for what you believe.

Harriet Tubman saved this man from being returned to slavery. Before she took actions, there was only talk about the situation. She took the leadership role to bring the necessary action needed.

Advocating for others is hard to do. Sometimes it requires you to put yourself at some risk. If you step out and speak out for someone else, you are now taking on the same problem or looked at the same as they are. If you feel strongly about something that seems wrong, take some actions. Actions speak louder than words. You could be the one that makes a difference. Let your love guide you to step up for someone else. Harriet Tubman showed what Love In Actions really means, compassionate leadership.

Activities

Discussion questions:

Alicia Garza, Patrisse Cullors, and Opal Tometi — created a Black-centered political will and movement building project called #BlackLivesMatter. It was in response to the acquittal of Trayvon Martin's murderer, George Zimmerman. Visit the Black Lives Matter website: https://blacklivesmatter.com/herstory/

1.   How are these 3 women representing the statement, "I Am Harriet Tubman"?
2.   Are Alicia, Patrisse, Opal servant leaders?

Take what they have done and check it through Mr. Robert Greenleaf "Best Test" for servant leaders. (page xii)

1.   Do those served grow as persons?
2.   Do they, while being served, become healthier, wiser, freer, more independent, or free, more likely themselves to become servants?
3.   What is the effect on the least privileged in society?
4.   Will they benefit, or at least, will they not be further deprived?

Journaling:

1. What organization have you heard about that fits the definition of advocacy (to support, campaign, sponsor, and believe in someone or something)?
2. Is there anything you would be willing to advocate for?
3. What unique talents do you have that you can use in love to advocate for a person or a cause?

Activities:

Use your creative talents to make a unique presentation about the cause or organization that you are passionate about.

Chapter 34

Leave Your Legacy

*I want history to remember me not as the first black woman to have
made a bid for the presidency of the United States, but as a black
woman who lived in the 20th century and who dared to be herself.
I want to be remembered as a catalyst for change in America.*

— *Shirley Chisholm*

Planting Seeds

When I was a little girl and a slave, my master forced me to
pick fruit from the trees, but I was forbidden to eat the fruit. I liked
apples, but if I got caught eating one, I was punished. I always said
I was going to grow some apples so that the children who came after
me could eat as many apples as they wanted. Now I have my own
apple orchard. I have apples and all you children can eat all you
want.

What I mean is, I want to help the children have a better life
by coming before them and making the changes in this country so
that they can live in freedom and be equal like the Bill of Rights and
Constitution say. I want them to be able to speak their minds, dream
big dreams, vote for their leaders, become leaders, and live truly
FREE. That's right, our bodies are free from bondage now, but not
all of us are free yet. We have to take the next step to learn that we
can do great things if we get our minds set on it. I always tried to
have a dollar or two to send back down South to two freedom
schools. See, I know children need to learn to read and write. They
can do so much these days. They even got some children thinking
about being doctors, lawyers, and teachers. I met one little boy who
wants to be a senator. Well, I couldn't do all that myself, but I want
to help them reach their dreams.

I never had any children of my own, but I took care of some
in my house in Auburn. When I got that house, it seemed like there

was always someone sick and poor finding their way to my door. I took them all in.

Next to my property was a beautiful stretch of land, twenty-five acres. I dreamed about how I could use this land. Part of it would be for farming and there would be plenty of land to build a large house for those poor souls that didn't have nowhere else to go. I always wanted to have this place and call it the John Brown Home. I looked out on this plot every day and prayed about it every day. Then one day the property came up for sale at an auction, and I was determined to get it.

I went to the auction, and I stooped down behind the crowd so no one would know who was bidding. The price started down pretty low. I kept bidding, upping it by $50.00 each bid. It got up to $1,250.00 before folks stopped bidding. I didn't have any money, but I had faith. The next day, I went to the bank, and I got a loan to buy the property using the property I just bought to secure the loan. There was more to my plan. I was in my eighties at this time. I was old, and I knew that someone else would be running the home. I gave the land to my church, the African Methodist Episcopal Zion Church. I knew they would do the right thing, but they didn't call it the John Brown Home. They insisted on naming it the Harriet Tubman Home. The doors opened in 1903. I moved in just a few years ago and I like it here. There is a sweet spirit in this place.

Leave a Legacy

Get started on your goals today. Know it will take time and possibly many steps. Stay determined. Keep on going forward. One action at a time is how Harriet Tubman left her legacy. She started as a young woman saving her own life. With courage and love, she returned and rescued dozens of other people. She never stopped serving. She never stopped finding ways to help other people. In each phase of her life, she took steps to make life better for others. She will be remembered for a legacy of service and Love In Actions.

Activities

Discussion question:

Shirley Anita Chisholm St. Hill was born November 30, 1924 she died on January 1, 2005. She was an American politician who, in 1968, became the first African American woman to be elected to the United States Congress. In 1972, she became the first African American candidate for a major-party nomination for President of the United States and the first woman to run for the Democratic Party's presidential nomination.

1.   Make a list of the ways Shirley Chisholm was a catalyst for change. (What has Shirley Chisholm started or strongly supported that has helped America get better for women?)

Journaling:

1. What type of legacy do you want to leave?
2. What steps can you take starting today that guide you toward your desired legacy?

Activities:

Get creative and show the world the kind of legacy you want to leave. This can be any art form. Express yourself as who you are and what you can do when you "plant your seeds."

GLOSSARY

accountability: being responsible to somebody or for something

advocate: to support or speak in favor of something

assertiveness: willingness to be forceful if a situation requires it confident in stating a position or claim

bodacious: It is used to describe something or someone as remarkable, impressive, or extraordinary, often with a sense of boldness, confidence, or audacity. In essence, it conveys a positive and enthusiastic quality.

character: good personal qualities that make somebody or something interesting or attractive. Somebody's public reputation

charismatic: possessing great powers of charm and influence

collaborator: the act of working together with one or more people in order to achieve something

determination: firmness of purpose, will, or intention

humility: the quality of being modest or respectful, humbleness, modesty, meekness, unassuming nature

influence: the power that somebody has to affect other people's thinking or action

inspirational: something that stimulates the human mind to creative thought

integrity: the quality of being faithful and holding onto high honest values, high moral principles, or professional standards

legacy: something that is handed down or remains from a previous generation or time

mentor: somebody, usually older and more experienced, who provides advice and support to a less experienced person. A mentor encourages this person's progress

people-oriented or people skills: Someone that enjoys working with or caring for people.

responsible: the state, fact, or position of being accountable to somebody or for something

self-empowerment: making a conscious decision to take charge of your life, your destiny Taking actions on your own behalf.

self-esteem: confidence in your own good points as a person

self-love: an appreciation for one's own well-being, happiness, respect for yourself and a demand that others respect you. Provide yourself with positive thoughts and kindness, trust and forgiveness.

synergy: the interaction or cooperation of two or more organizations, substances, or other agents to produce a combined effect greater than the sum of their separate effects.

visionary: somebody who sees or imagines what the future might look like

RESOURCES

Bradford, Sarah H. *Scenes In The Life Of Harriet Tubman*. Auburn: William G. Wise, 1869. Library of Congress Subject Headings, 21st edition, 1998 The University of North Carolina at Chapel Hill Library, 2000

Bradford, Sarah H. *Harriet, The Moses of Her People*. New York: Published for the author by Geo. R. Lockwood and Son, 1886. Library of Congress Subject Headings, 21st edition, 1998 Academic Affairs Library, The University of North Carolina at Chapel Hill Library 1995

Motivate The Masses – Lisa Nichols1 - Motivating The Masses ...https://motivatingthemasses.com

Brainyquote.com

Beckwithhttps://www.goodreads.com/author/quotes/559322 " "Michael Bernard Beckwith"

Conrad, Earl. *Harriet Tubman: Negro Soldier and Abolitionist*. International Publishers Co., Inc., 1942, fifth printing 1973.

Larson, Kate Clifford. *Bound for the Promised Land, Harriet Tubman Portrait of an American Hero*. New York: The Random House Publishing Group, 2004.

Pictures courtesy of the US Library of Congress *Photograph of Harriet Tubman*. , 1911. Photograph. https://www.loc.gov/item/rbcmiller002657/. Powelson, Benjamin F, photographer. *Portrait of Harriet Tubman / Powelson, photographer, 77 Genesee St., Auburn, New York*. New York, 1868. [Auburn, N.Y.: Benjamin Powelson, or 1869]

Photograph. https://www.loc.gov/item/2018645050/.

Visit our website for more resources: www.karolvbrown.com

Wikipedia for biographic information https://en.wikipedia.org/

A LETTER FROM THE AUTHOR

Hello, beautiful Goddess. I dearly hope that as you were guided through the Harriet Tubman Way, you have found your beauty, your joy, and your unique gifts through developing your self-love.

I want to share a story with you about this book. I self-published my first book about Harriet Tubman in 2013, "30 Lessons in Love, Leadership and Legacy from Harriet Tubman". It's similar to this book, and I was proud of it. However, with more historically well-researched biographies about Harriet Tubman, the number of people she rescued and the number of trips she traveled changed. They decreased from 300 people and 19 trips to 70 people and 13 trips. Because I considered my book nonfiction, I wanted to share Harriet Tubman's true stories as I learned them. I felt I needed to update that book.

So, I set my goal to publish a second edition. I kept setting this goal and resetting it. Years went by. But I never got to it until my life changed. That's another story, in another book. Only after there were major changes in my life that I set out determined to rewrite the book. I thought I would highlight servant-leadership concepts more in the second edition. Finally, I had a finished draft to submit to my publisher. But it changed due to not being able to use some quotes on servant leadership that I wanted to use. So, I decided it was time to do the book I thought would come much later.

The book for girls. Harriet Tubman's stories that I have told hundreds of times, to me, were teaching self-love. I felt, our girls need to learn to love themselves. Finally, I released my book, "The Harriet Tubman Way, An Inspirational Guide for Self-Love, Empowerment, and Legendary Leadership for Girls", in Dayton, Ohio as the speaker for the League of Women Voters celebration of Women's Equality Day, August 26, 2022.

When I read the finished book, I realized that, although I wrote it for 5th and 6th grade girls, I needed to love myself more too. I now say I wrote this book for all girls and women.

What is the Harriet Tubman Way? It is a spiritual connection to the divine in all of us through Self-Love, Self-Care, and Self-Empowerment. It is about leaving a legacy, like Harriet Tubman. A legacy that will be admired for 100+ years after your death. We, by speaking the name, Harriet Tubman, are stretching remembrance of her legendary life further and further out to more generations that will never let her name fade in significance.

One more part of this story I want to be shared in this edition of this Harriet Tubman Way book. This book you are reading is not the original book under this title that was released in 2022. The other book is the same name, same cover except the font on this book is different. My picture on the back is different and this letter is not in it.

I was blessed with a network of beautiful mature women, mothers and grandmothers who met with me on Wednesdays starting in October 2023. We went through each chapter of this book and discussed how we each would share it with the younger women and girls in our neighborhoods, churches, and families. It was during these sessions that the comments from the women made this book change and become so much better! Members of this group gave me such wonderful feedback. We had fun watching and discussing music videos to match the theme and sharing wisdom and experiences. We all left our Zoom calls feeling inspired. One major comment was that there were too many quotes from men in the book. At first, I defended my inclusion of the men. "The girls can learn from the men too.", But these comments led me to review my chapter quotes from their perspective. They were Right! I quoted more men than women!

Where was MY MIND when I selected the quotes? (Well, that is in the other book too.) I realized what I was thinking a few days later. This book started as a revision of 30 Lessons book where I had 31 quotes from all kinds of people whom I admired. But I decided to make a new book, with all the quotes from black people. Why the change? Because I want children in the 5th grade to read this book and learn about more black people than Harriet Tubman. So, I matched the quotes with the topics not realizing the number of quotes from black men. Thanks to the ladies' comments from our Wednesday group, I decided to change all the quotes from men in the Harriet Tubman Way book. Now, in this edition, all the quotes are from black women. It's not that there was anything wrong with quoting the men, they were excellent matches for the chapters. But now it is more meaningful to its purpose. As I was searching for quotes, I was enjoying it so much! I was learning more and more about so many beautiful black women and this book is going to teach our girls about these women too! Women in different age groups, different life stories, and so much wisdom! You see, God has big plans for this book, this curriculum, and my movement, "Girls United by Love!"

There are so many links in the chain of this story. The challenges I have experienced in the last few years have helped me strengthen and hold on to my faith that everything will be okay. Just hold on. As Harriet would say, "Keep On Going!

"This moment right now, while I am writing this letter to you, is only because of all the delays that have taken place and the women who shared in our "Safe Space", their honest opinions, their truth. All that has made me better, so I could make this book better. Thank you, ladies!

I have been blessed to release this book again, as an honor to black women who have the "Spirit of Harriet Tubman", a Legendary Beautiful Black Bodacious Boss Woman! Say it with me, "I AM HARRIET TUBMAN".

My Beautiful Souls, in Your Beautiful Unique Gift Boxes, I LOVE YOU!

Thank You Quippy Quill for publishing this new edition.

Blessings,

Karol V. Brown

PS: I want to give you a suggestion. If you have the original copy of this book with the quotes from some amazing black men that I admire, KEEP IT! It's going to be worth a lot of money one day!

ABOUT THE AUTHOR

Karol V. Brown

Karol V. Brown, a dedicated professional with a Bachelor of Science degree and a Master of Public Health, is certified as a Lisa Nichols Transformational Trainer, and skilled in Emotion Code Energy Medicine. Based in Washington State, Karol is a seasoned health educator, accomplished author, and captivating storytelling artist. With over 23 years of experience, she has passionately shared the inspiring stories and wisdom of Harriet Tubman.

Karol is the author of two impactful books, "30 Lessons in Love, Leadership, and Legacy from Harriet Tubman" and "The Harriet Tubman Way: An Inspirational Guide to Self-Love, Empowerment, and Legendary Leadership for Girls." Additionally, she has co-authored three other books, namely "Rise Up" with Lisa Nichols, "Live Love, Prosper," with Authors Who Care, and together with professional storytellers, "How to Be A Storyteller."

Specializing in interactive storytelling workshops and compelling speaking engagements, Karol focuses on empowering young girls and women to discover their inner strength and potential, drawing inspiration from the remarkable life of Harriet Tubman. Her presentations center around essential themes such as self-love, peace, joy, gratitude, determination, and imagination.

Figure 9 www.harriettubman3lc.com

www.ingramcontent.com/pod-product-compliance
Lightning Source LLC
Chambersburg PA
CBHW021641120626
46545CB00002B/648

* 9 7 8 1 9 6 1 6 7 7 2 0 3 *